*Historical Association Studies*

Lloyd George

# WITHDRAWN

The Historical Association, founded in 1906, brings together people who share an interest in, and love for, the past. It aims to further the study and teaching of history at all levels: teacher and student, amateur and professional. This is one of over 100 publications available at preferential rates to members. Membership also includes journals at generous discounts and gives access to courses, conferences, tours and regional and local activities. Full details are available from The Secretary, The Historical Association, 59a Kennington Park Road, London SE11 4JH, telephone: 071–735 3901.

# Lloyd George

*Chris Wrigley*

**BLACKWELL**
*Oxford UK & Cambridge USA*

Copyright © C. J. Wrigley, 1992

The right of Christopher John Wrigley to be identified as author of this work has been asserted in accordance with the Copyright, Designs and Patents Act 1988.

First published 1992

Blackwell Publishers
108 Cowley Road, Oxford OX4 1JF, UK

238 Main Street, Suite 501
Cambridge, MA 02142, USA

*British Library Cataloguing in Publication Data*
A CIP catalogue record for this book is available from the British Library.

*Library of Congress Cataloging-in-Publication Data*
Wrigley, Chris.
    Lloyd George/Chris Wrigley.
        p.    cm. — (Historical Association studies)
    Includes bibliographical references and index.
    ISBN 0−631−18065−6. (hbk)    ISBN 0−631−16608−4 (pbk)
        1. Lloyd George, David, 1865−1945.    2. Prime ministers − Great
    Britain − Biography.    3. Great Britain − Politics and
    government − 1837−1901.    4. Great Britain − Politics and
    government − 1901−1936.    5. Great Britain − Politics and
    government − 1936−1945.    I. Title.    II. Series.
    DA566.9.L5W756    1992
    941.083′092−dc20                                                    91−44031
    [B]                                                                        CIP

Typeset in Ehrhardt
by Setrite Typesetters Ltd, Hong Kong
Printed in Great Britain by T.J. Press (Padstow) Ltd, Padstow, Cornwall.

This book is printed on acid-free paper

# *Contents*

# *Acknowledgements*

I am grateful to Professor Kenneth O. Morgan and Professor Muriel Chamberlain (the series editor) for their valuable advice.

# 1

# *Introduction*

David Lloyd George (1863–1945) is one of the most colourful figures of modern British political history. His rise to the premiership from a relatively humble background was depicted (not least by him) as the British equivalent of the American dream of 'log cabin to White House'. Or, as he himself put it at the start of his successful parliamentary by-election campaign in 1890, 'the day of the cottage-bred man has at last dawned' (*Carnarvon Herald*, 28 March 1890).

Lloyd George, like Disraeli, is one of the great outsiders of what has usually been an *English* political system. Lord Blake, writing before James Callaghan's premiership, observed, 'The fact remains ... that in spite of all the democratization of the past hundred years there has only been one occupant of Number Ten Downing Street since Disraeli, who neither inherited substantial wealth nor went to a famous public school, nor attended an ancient university – and that was Lloyd George, almost as much a "foreigner" as Disraeli himself' (Blake, 1966, p. 763).

Lloyd George's political career began as the voice of Welsh rural radicalism, as the enemy of landlords, especially English ones, and of all inherited privilege. In his early parliamentary years he tried to be the Parnell of Wales. Later, at times invoking the tradition of Cobden and Bright, he condemned the way that the British Empire crushed the small Boer states in the war of 1899–1902. Yet as Prime Minister between 1916 and 1922 he governed with the support of the Conservative Party, and for periods his position depended on the support of the Imperial pro-consul, Lord Milner, the aristocrat and former Viceroy of India, Lord Curzon, and the 'no surrender' Ulsterman, Sir

Edward Carson. His ascent to the premiership in December 1916 was linked to belief in his total commitment to victory, the policy of 'the knock-out blow' to Germany. He ended the First World War seen by millions as the saviour of the British Empire, the 'Man Who Won the War' — in much the same way as Pitt the Elder was in the mid-eighteenth century and Winston Churchill after the Second World War.

Lloyd George's accession to the premiership involved the displacement of his own party leader, Herbert Henry Asquith. This, together with his decision to fight the 1918 General Election in harness with the Conservatives (with the resulting rout of the Asquithian Liberal leaders) and his scant regard for many of the old tenets of Liberalism, were seen as dark crimes by many traditional Liberals. In the eyes of many of his former most loyal supporters, 'the People's Champion' had gone the way of Joseph Chamberlain — into the arms of the Tory enemy.

And yet, after his fall from office in 1922 Lloyd George joined neither the Conservative nor the Labour parties. As Charles Masterman, a Liberal who had been estranged from Lloyd George since 1915, confessed to his wife in the mid-1920s, 'I've fought him as hard as anyone but I have to confess, when Lloyd George came back to the party, ideas came back to the party' (Masterman, 1939, pp. 345–6). Lloyd George was quick to take up new ideas and to try to adapt Liberalism to the circumstances of the 1920s and 1930s. He supported both the Labour minority governments of 1924 and 1929–31, deeming Labour to be a lesser evil then than the Conservatives.

After the longest continuous period of Cabinet office in recent British history (December 1905–October 1922) Lloyd George ended his parliamentary career with a long spell away from the ministerial benches (1922–45), though from at least 1922 to 1931 he was a major political force to be reckoned with, and one whom Stanley Baldwin and James Ramsay MacDonald feared.

In the eyes of his Radical nonconformist supporters Lloyd George's zenith had been in the pre-war Liberal governments. For the electorate at large, the high point of his career was the peacemaking in Paris in 1919, when he was one of the world statesmen redrawing the map of Europe, just as emperors and aristocrats had done a century before at the Congress of Vienna. His subsequent career was a long aftermath to that triumph.

From an early stage his career attracted strongly pro or anti accounts. Before the First World War the favourable included two four-volume

2

biographies (Du Parcq, 1912—13; Edwards, 1913) and one short Welsh-language life (J. T. Davies, 1910). Herbert du Parcq, who was given access to many family papers by Lloyd George's brother, declared in his book that 'there is no reason why a chronicler may not follow in the tracks of an heroic progress as yet incomplete, and glean upon the way for the admirer of his present triumphs such records as are extant of its past efforts and achievements'. Lloyd George's later 'progress', however, was to alienate du Parcq, as it did so many other pre-war admirers. Watkin Davies who, like Edwards and Beriah Gwynfe Evans (author of *The Life Romance of Lloyd George*), was a Liberal newspaperman, published in 1939 one of the best accounts of Lloyd George's career before 1914. But it is notable that he never completed a second volume, and in the first complained that with the Great War the Welsh foundations on which Lloyd George's career had been built were crumbling 'and the consequence was the purposeless career of the years after 1919' (W. W. Davies, 1939, p. 281).

On the other hand there were remarkably virulent assessments by Unionists before and after the war. G. E. Raine, who had been an unsuccessful Unionist parliamentary candidate, published a vigorous attack on him at the time of the Marconi Scandal ('he is all emotions and no balance': Raine, 1913, p. 9) and at the time of the Land Campaign followed it with a further one ('Mr George embodies in himself most of the Plagues of Egypt of our day': Raine, 1914, p. xiii). After the war there were similar effusions from the Tory Right, such as *The Man Who Didn't Win the War: an exposure of Lloyd Georgism* (1923) by 'Centurion' (which appeared originally in the *National Review*).

But what was more significant was that many of the critical books after 1922 were written by Liberals, some of whom had formerly supported him. At the time of the Liberal reunion J. M. Robertson condemned Lloyd George's political integrity and rejected any notion of his becoming Leader of the Liberal Party, asking, 'Does Mr Lloyd George meet the moral requirements any more than did Chamberlain?' (Robertson, 1923, p. 22). Sir Charles Mallet in his biography, published when Lloyd George was still Leader of the Liberal Party, contrasted Lloyd George's qualities, much to his detriment, with '[t]he character which Mr Gladstone bore and the standards of conduct which he left us'. Mallet's verdict that Lloyd George's return to office would be 'serious for Liberals who still place some value on principle in public life' (Mallet, 1930, pp. 309—13) was in essence that expounded by Asquith's followers and by his family in numerous autobiographies

3

and books for two decades after Lloyd George's death. While Asquith's papers were available and books appeared that were sympathetic to the view of Asquith as 'the last of the Romans' (that is, before the barbarians took over), Lloyd George's papers were closed until the mid-1960s. They had been bought by Lord Beaverbrook in late 1949 from Lloyd George's second wife, the former Frances Stevenson, and were used only by Frank Owen (1954) and by Beaverbrook himself for two of his books (1956, 1963).

In the two decades after his death, Lloyd George's reputation depended on worthy but dull biographies by Thomson (1948) and Jones (1951). A lively account, but one limited in its choice of themes, was given by Frank Owen (1954) who as a Liberal MP (1929–31) had supported Lloyd George and opposed the formation of the National Government; later he was editor of the *Evening Standard*. These books were overshadowed by sensational allegations by his elder son about his sex life (R. Lloyd George, 1960) and by a vigorous debunking of his reputation as a whole by D. McCormick in *The Mask of Merlin* (1963).

The scholarly reassessment of Lloyd George's career was started by A. J. P. Taylor and Kenneth O. Morgan. Taylor focused on Lloyd George's role in two major public lectures (Taylor, 1959 and 1961); and in his volume in the *Oxford History of England* he delivered the judgement that Lloyd George was 'the greatest prime minister of the century' (Taylor, 1965, p. 87). Morgan marked the centenary of Lloyd George's birth by exploring the theme of 'Welsh Radical as World Statesman' (Morgan, 1963a) and made his initial contribution to the reassessment of Lloyd George by carefully locating Lloyd George's early career in Welsh society and politics (Morgan, 1963b). Both authors have done justice to Lloyd George, and it would be fair to say that with their work the pendulum of interpretation swung back considerably in his favour.

In the past quarter of a century reassessments of most aspects of his life have been facilitated by the opening of many (but not all) of the collections central to his life and political career. The main collection of Lloyd George papers, which were housed in the Beaverbrook Library from 1967 to 1975, are now located in the House of Lords Record Office. While Honorary Director of the Beaverbrook Library, Taylor edited both Frances Stevenson's diary and her correspondence with Lloyd George (1971b and 1975) as well as a collection of essays on Lloyd George arising from early research by scholars in that Library's various collections of private papers (1971a). Many

Lloyd George family letters and other material relating to his life are deposited in the National Library of Wales, Aberystwyth. Kenneth O. Morgan has edited a selection of Lloyd George's correspondence with Margaret, his first wife (Morgan, 1973). In addition, from the mid-1960s onwards various public records, such as Cabinet minutes and papers, have become available at the Public Record Office.

These recently available records have been used in a new series of valuable biographies which began with Kenneth O. Morgan's short study (1974) and continued with a large single volume by Peter Rowland (1975) and a book on Lloyd George's career up to 1914 by Don Cregier (1976). More recent additions include Martin Pugh's brief reassessment (1988) and a collection of essays marking the centenary of Lloyd George's election to Parliament (Loades, 1991). These primary sources have also been utilized by the writers of the two multi-volume biographies which have been a long time in the writing: John Grigg's lively, original and attractively written work (three volumes to date – 1973, 1978 and 1985 – with possibly two volumes to come), and Bentley Gilbert's very detailed study (one volume so far – 1987 – with possibly two more to follow). In addition, since the mid-1970s there has been a steady flow of monographs.

The present book draws on much of this recent research into Lloyd George's career to provide a brief assessment of the man who Lord Blake once described as 'an enigma to the historian' (Blake, 1952, p. 42).

# 2

# The Welsh Nonconformist Politician

The roots of Lloyd George's political attitudes lay in the late 1870s and the 1880s: the period of the last conflicts between Disraeli and Gladstone and of the Liberal Party splits over the issue of Home Rule. His starting point was in the midst of the nonconformist politics of North Wales.

After Lloyd George's death Churchill said of him, 'He was the greatest Welshman which that unconquerable race has produced since the age of the Tudors' (409 *H. C. Deb. 5s*, 1380, 28 March 1945). On the centenary of his birth Kenneth O. Morgan wrote that 'his ties with Wales provide one – and perhaps the only – constant element throughout his kaleidoscopic political career' (Morgan, 1963a, p. 10). His Welsh origins were indeed a powerful influence on his political concerns and manoeuvres, albeit a diminishing one even from the late 1890s. He remained well aware of the need to maintain and foster his connections with his early political base of Welsh Liberalism, at least until 1915; and after his fall from office in 1922 he remained the favourite son of North Wales throughout the inter-war period.

David Lloyd George was actually born in England, at 5, New York Place, Robert Street, Chorlton-upon-Medlock, Manchester, on 17 January 1863. But his childhood time in England was of short duration. His family moved back to Wales when he was four months old. He was the second child and elder son of a Welsh couple: William George, a schoolmaster, and Elizabeth (Betsy) Lloyd who, before marriage, had been first a domestic servant, then a lady's companion. After a year as a tenant farmer in Pembrokeshire, William George died of pneumonia. Betsy George, then pregnant, returned to her birthplace, Llanystumdwy, with her daughter Mary Ellen and her son David Lloyd. The lived with her mother Rebecca Llwyd, and her younger brother Richard, who together maintained the family shoemaking business. This was sufficiently flourishing to support them as well as Betsy and her three children, and to employ two men. After Rebecca Llwyd died in June 1868 Richard kept the shoemaking business going until ill-health forced him to give it up in 1880. As the *South Wales New*'s obituary (1 March 1917) of Richard Lloyd commented, 'There was no suggestion of want or poverty about Mr Lloyd George's early days, but it was a hard, thrifty life, and provided a mental, moral and religious discipline.' It added of Uncle Lloyd's shop that it 'was described as the "hub of the village", where folks met to dicuss the affairs of this world and the next. It was a forcing house of Welsh Radicalism.'

Richard Lloyd, like his father before him, was an unpaid nonconformist minister. From 1859 until his death he was a pastor for a Baptist sect, the Disciples of Christ, which believed that as all are equal in the eyes of God there should be no formal offices or ministers. David Lloyd George was brought up on the Bible by his uncle and was accustomed to the skilful and powerful oratory of his uncle's sermons. On 12 December 1880 he wrote in his diary:

> Uncle Lloyd splendid and all through his sermon there were the most startling hits, and the peroration swept everything before him. The audience's feelings drowned in tears. Never heard anything like it. (George, 1958, p. 22)

For David, Richard Lloyd filled the gap left by the early death of his father. Though David and his younger brother William referred to Uncle Lloyd in jest as 'the Bishop', they respected his strong moral character and his judgement. Yet there was a certain ambiguity in David's attitude to his uncle. He was the apple of Uncle Lloyd's eye – and the charm for which Lloyd George was later famous was given early exercise on his uncle. Yet at times there was within him a revolt against the elder man's firm certainties, involving Christian faith, sabbatarianism and, briefly, even Gladstonian Liberal politics.

Being so favoured by such an impressive figure as Uncle Lloyd gave David Lloyd George confidence, but it also encouraged him to expect to be the centre of attention and the recipient of assistance from others. William later observed, 'Whether this unrestrained admiration was wholly good for the lad upon whom it was lavished, and

7

indeed for the man who evolved out of him, is a matter upon which opinion may differ' (George, 1958, p. 33). Lloyd George grew up in a patriarchal household, where the first-born male received much attention and where David's mother and sister rarely entered the limelight. Great sacrifices were made by his uncle – both of money and time – to enable him and William to train as solicitors. Once they had qualified, David soon put his interests first, ruthlessly using his brother to enable him to run a private solicitors' practice while at the same time indulging in the expensive business of politics. David was lucky that his brother William was willing to work hard and selflessly, taking on the responsibility of providing the main income for the family after Richard Lloyd had given up the shoemaking business and they had moved to Criccieth.

Similarly, Lloyd George expected his interests to be uppermost in marriage. He was very explicit about this in his comments to Margaret Owen before their marriage, as was Winston Churchill with Clementine Hozier. Some months ahead of their marriage in January 1888 Lloyd George wrote:

> I am of opinion that women's function is to soothe and sympathise and not to amuse. Men's lives are a perpetual conflict. The life I have mapped out will be so especially – as lawyer and politician. Woman's function is to pour oil on the wounds – to heal the bruises of spirit received in past conflicts and to stimulate a renewed exertion. (Morgan, 1973, p. 19)

He was even blunter in an earlier letter:

> It comes to this, my supreme idea is to get on. To this idea I shall sacrifice everything – except, I trust, honesty. I am prepared to thrust even love itself under the wheels of my Juggernaut if it obstructs the way. (Morgan, 1973, p. 14)

Later, Lloyd George was to be angered by his wife's wish to remain with their young family in Criccieth rather than spend the parliamentary sessions in London.

This home background may help to explain why Lloyd George maintained even fewer friendships than is normal in politics. Later he was to treat devoted political supporters, such as Charles Masterman and Christopher Addison, in an insensitive and self-centred manner. It was as though he expected selfless support from others as a right. As for his few friendships, these were mostly politically opportune. Thus Herbert Lewis as a Welsh MP provided a means by which he maintained links with Welsh Liberalism, and George Riddell as a newspaper proprietor belonged to a class of men to whom Lloyd George naturally gravitated. Yet like Winston Churchill, another of his few friends, David Lloyd George's life was consumed by an interest in politics; so it was likely that those whose company he enjoyed would be linked to public affairs.

Lloyd George was bitten by the political bug early: at least by the age of 17, when he canvassed on behalf of the Liberal candidate for the Carnarvonshire seat in the 1880 General Election. He was deeply involved, as the firm of solicitors to which he was articled acted as Liberal agent. The Liberal victory in that election was a great triumph: the seat had been held by Lord Penrhyn and his son since 1841, except when it was won once by the Liberals in 1868. Lloyd George was euphoric, writing in his diary on 7 April 1880:

> Scenes of wildest enthusiasm. Evan butcher [sic] got hold of donkey that was passing and shouted in its ears that its brother had lost. Bonfires and fireballs. ... A great blow to landlord terrorism, and quite as great a triumph for the ballot. (George, 1976, p. 94)

From early on he had ambitions to make his name nationally and not just in North Wales. His first visit to London included a trip to the Houses of Parliament on 12 November 1881. He wrote in his diary, 'I will not say but that I eyed the assembly in the spirit similar to that in which William the Conqueror eyed England on his visit to Edward the Confessor, as the region of his future domain' (Du Parcq, 1912–13, p. 40). In early 1884 he was confiding in his diary, even before he sat his final law examinations, that he wanted more from life than to be a prosperous Welsh solicitor. He hoped 'to pursue my great ambition – to be eminent as a public speaker', and added that to achieve his 'higher object – fame – London is the place for that' (George, 1976, p. 115).

A striking feature of Lloyd George's career is that he made his own way in politics. He was not born into political circles, as were Winston Churchill and Arthur Balfour. Though he attracted the attention and then the support of influential Welsh Radicals such as Thomas Gee, he was not directly helped into Parliament and later to the front bench by patrons, as were many of his generation. He benefited from no 'old school' or Oxbridge connections. He later commented, 'It is a terrible struggle, the struggle to secure recognition' (Riddell, 1933b, p. 35). He made his mark primarily through his abilities as a public speaker and through his ardent espousal of the causes then uppermost in the Radical politics of North Wales.

Lloyd George developed his oratory at local debating societies, through preaching and by giving temperance lectures. He worked in Portmadoc for the solicitors Breese, Jones and Casson from July 1878 until the end of 1884. He became a member of Portmadoc Debating Society on 28 November 1881, soon after his first visit to Parliament, and attended meetings regularly during the next two years and intermittently for several years thereafter. He also joined the Criccieth Debating Society and became its Chairman in 1885, the year in which he opened his own solicitor's office in the town. Like others of a nonconformist background, such as Arthur Henderson in Northumberland (the future Labour Party leader, who was also born in 1863), Lloyd George enhanced his speaking skills and made himself known more widely through being a lay preacher and a temperance lecturer. By the mid-1880s he was clearly a very accomplished speaker. He noted in his diary on 28 March 1885 of his performance at a Welsh disestablishment meeting, 'Spoke between forty and forty-five minutes with much ease, and in the end with much fire; getting into the *hwyl* [fervour] without knowing it when declaiming about liberty' (Du Parcq, 1912, p. 45). His public speaking skills were also enhanced by his court appearances as a solicitor.

Lloyd George's profession also gave him opportunities to make a name for himself as a champion of Welsh working people against privilege. His acting on behalf of working men charged with poaching was one example of this. His greatest triumph came in 1888 when he successfully defended a group of dissenters who, with nonconformist rites, had buried an old quarryman next to his daughter's grave in an Anglican churchyard in spite of the opposition of the rector. In winning the Llanfrothen burial case Lloyd George exposed the pig-headedness of the rector and the partiality of the English judge. As William George later wrote, 'This case put the firm of Lloyd George and George, and particularly Dafydd, well on the Law Map of Wales' (George, 1958, p. 143). More than that, it made Lloyd George a hero among nonconformists.

While his speaking abilities were an essential ingredient in his emergence as a parliamentary candidate, they were not sufficient. Lloyd George gained his local prominence through hard and enthusiastic work as a Liberal activist. He was quick to join many of the pressure groups which formed a part of Welsh Liberalism in the 1880s. From 1885 he was a regular speaker on behalf of the Liberation

10

Society (which campaigned for the disestablishment of the Church of England and the Church in Wales). Also he spoke, in all probability from 1885, for the Farmers' Union of North Wales which campaigned for better tenancy terms and reduced rents (Gilbert, 1987, pp. 51–3). From his Farmers' Union activities came an invitation for him to speak with Michael Davitt, the organizer of the Irish Land League, at Blaenau Ffestiniog on 12 February 1886. The flair he displayed in moving the vote of thanks to Davitt both enhanced his growing reputation as a young man with a promising political future and marked him as being well on the Left of Welsh Liberalism. Lloyd George concluded his speech on this occasion by urging, 'When a land league was started for Wales, he hoped they would all join it' (Du Parcq, 1912, pp. 76–7). Not surprisingly, he went on to be active in the anti-tithe campaign which spread through Wales later in 1886. That year he took on the role of Secretary of the South Carnarvonshire branch of the Anti-tithe League, and spoke on the subject at many meetings.

Yet for all his single-minded, energetic devotion to making his mark in politics, in several respects Lloyd George's views did not fit neatly into the mould of Radical nonconformity. While Arthur Henderson travelled far and wide as a lay preacher and his reputation in this role furthered his chances of a parliamentary nomination in the north-east of England, there can be no doubt that his faith played a central role in his life. Whatever else may be ambiguous about Lloyd George, it is very clear that he did not share Uncle Lloyd's simple, abiding and deep faith.

There are different views as to his faith. Bentley Gilbert has argued that it appears to have slipped away over a period of some years, with the loss being especially marked in the time after he left his Llanystumdwy home in 1878 to board in Portmadoc (Gilbert, 1987, pp. 35–7). This picture can also be derived from Frances Stevenson's diaries (Taylor, 1971b, pp. 77, 276, 288). Indeed, in the autumn of 1915 Lloyd George gave her a detailed account of how, at the age of 11, he had realized that 'religion, as he was taught it, was a mockery and a sham'; and how for some seven years the subject was a source of mental distress. But perhaps, in such discussions with his mistress, he was both reminiscing and reassuring her as to the free-thinking nature of his nonconformity.

In contrast to Gilbert, Ian Machin has suggested that it is likely that Lloyd George's faith waxed and waned over the years, more like Charles Stuart Parnell's experience than Joseph Chamberlain's sudden

11

and outright loss of faith (Machin, 1991, p. 36). Certainly, throughout his life Lloyd George maintained his Baptist credentials, at least on the surface. Shortly before the Second World War Watkin Davies wrote:

> In his allegiance to the religious interests of his boyhood he has never wavered; and although his theology would no longer be considered orthodox by the old Llanystumdwy neighbours, there has been no falling away on his part from any of the essentials of the Free Churchman's creed. Chamberlain was lost to Unitarianism, as Asquith was to Congregationalism; but Lloyd George is still in every sense of the term a Baptist. (W. W. Davies, 1939, p. 217)

There is much truth in this regarding his outward faith; but as to his inner faith, by the First World War one may be sceptical. However, having been reared in such a God-fearing house as that of Richard Lloyd the habits of mind remained, and during the rest of his life he dug deep into the rich ground of biblical tales and imagery for his speeches. Nevertheless, in respecting nonconformist sensibilities and appealing for nonconformist support there were tensions between what he professed and what he still believed. Much the same could be said of temperance, an issue he continued to emphasize in his early parliamentary career and one of which he was very aware, even after the First World War.

While an articled clerk in Portmadoc, Lloyd George also displayed interests that were unusual for a Radical activist. Under the influence of Randall Casson, the principal of his firm, Lloyd George joined the Volunteers in 1882. His diary suggests that he enjoyed going to camps and drinking beer and port (in spite of his temperance pledge of the same year), but — aptly enough — he was not good at drill. Du Parcq, who was given access to Lloyd George's early diaries by William George for his 1912 biography, was clearly taken aback that his Radical hero should have 'found time for the pursuit of arms', which he observed was 'an interest ... rather out of harmony with his other pursuits of the time' (Du Parcq, 1912, p. 40).

As well as disapproving of such traits in his favourite nephew, Uncle Lloyd was also concerned by Lloyd George's espousal of Joseph Chamberlain's cause in the immediate aftermath of the Liberal Party debates on Home Rule in 1886. Lloyd George greatly admired Chamberlain during the 1880−5 Gladstone administration, writing in a local newspaper in October 1884 that:

'Mr Chamberlain is unquestionably the future leader of the people.... He is convinced that the aristocracy stands in the way of the development of the rights of man, and he says so unflinchingly, though he be howled at as an ill-mannered demagogue by the whole kennelry of gorged aristocracy, and of their fawning minions. (*North Wales Observer*, 17 October 1884)

For him, Chamberlain was very much the coming man, a Radical middle-class man who had risen to the top of Liberal politics by his own energies and who offered policies which could excite working-class voters. During the 1885 General Election, Lloyd George despondently noted Tory victories and complained, 'there is no cry for the towns. Humdrum Liberalism won't win elections.' When there were Liberal victories in county seats he commented, 'Am convinced that this is all due to Chamberlain's speeches. Gladstone had no programme that would draw at all' (diary entries, 25 November and 4 December, 1885; see Du Parcq, 1912, pp. 48–9).

That Lloyd George came close to following Chamberlain when the Liberal Party divided over Home Rule in 1886 should not be seen with hindsight as an early sign of cross-party inclinations on Lloyd George's part. Among the most Radical of Welsh Liberal activists there was a certain kudos in lamenting Gladstone's lack of urgency to do something for Wales when compared with his apparently permanent priority to remedy Irish ills. They also regretted his lack of a social programme. Lloyd George was trying to make his mark as a thrusting Radical with an irreverent attitude to the concerns of the older generation of leading Liberal politicians in North Wales. When in June 1886 he offered such support as lay within his 'limited power' to Tom Ellis for the Merioneth parliamentary candidature he wrote that he did so as he felt Ellis was 'destined to rescue Wales from the grip of respectable dummyism' (Lloyd George to Ellis, 12 June 1886: Ellis Papers, f.678).

However, in the late 1880s and early 1890s Lloyd George was often trying to go too fast for the often staid nonconformity of North Wales. At a meeting of leading North Wales Liberals at Bangor over the Easter weekend of 1886, Lloyd George found himself in a minority of one when he took Chamberlain's side against Gladstone. Other than Thomas Gee, there were few people of political weight whom Lloyd George respected who came out on the Chamberlain side. Uncle Lloyd's faith in Gladstone remained undimmed. He wrote in his diary on 14 April 1886, 'What a pity Chamberlain is astray', and later noted that one of his nephew's staunchest supporters in Criccieth had warned him 'that D.Ll.G must be careful or he would be accused of being against the Party' (George, 1976, pp. 132–3). Lloyd George, whose political antennae were always sensitive to changes in political mood, soon distanced himself from any commitment to Radical Unionism.

But his attitude to Irish Home Rule always remained qualified. After Lloyd George died, Professor W. G. S. Adams, who had been head of Lloyd George's Prime Ministerial Secretariat, reflected on the ambiguities of his attitude to Ireland:

It must all go far back in history ... how far was he a Gladstonian? and that, even with W. E. G., went through its phases – though W. E. G. was a crusader for Home Rule for Ireland and I question if L. G. ever was. Yet I should expect that Federal Home Rule – and Joe Chamberlain was going that way – was nearer to L. G.'s real desire. But other things baulked it, and he did not feel the crusader for it in him as the old man had done for his Home Rule ... I remember feeling as I talked with him that when I got below the surface of his mind there was this deep primitive 'No Pope here' of Ulster – something that stirred depths in his makeup and that explains despite all his efforts to get over it ... the settlement with Ulster. (Adams to T. Jones, 31 January 1948; Thomas Jones Papers A2/24)

For the young Lloyd George the main appeal of Ireland was as a model for nationalist demands, especially disestablishment and agrarian reforms (Morgan, 1989, p. 84). Thus in 1889, when he had been selected as a parliamentary candidate, he spoke of Ireland as 'a college for Europe – a college of liberty, which taught how every wronged and oppressed nationality might secure justice and redress', before going on to say that he felt that Wales was like a horse that came third in a horse show, just 'highly commended' by the Liberal leadership (*Carnarvon Herald*, 15 February 1889).

Lloyd George first made public his parliamentary ambitions when still in his early twenties. This was in spite of the fact that his firm's finances were not then strong enough to fund him as an MP (payment of MPs did not come about until 1911). Before the 1886 General Election Lloyd George made it known that he was a potential candidate for the Liberal nomination, not only for Carnarvon District but also for the safer Liberal seat of Merioneth, should Tom Ellis decide not to stand. Breese had been the Liberal agent for Merioneth, and Lloyd George had made many contacts in the constituency both when he worked for Breese and later when he had his own practice (Price, 1975a, p. 293). The Liberals of his home constituency retained their existing MP, Sir T. L. Jones Parry, as candidate, but he lost his seat by 136 votes to the Conservative candidate Edmund Swetenham. In Merioneth Ellis did win the Liberal nomination and went on to hold the seat in the General Election.

The defeat of Jones Parry left an opening for a new Liberal candidate for Carnarvon District. In September 1887 Lloyd George readily accepted an invitation to go on the panel of possible candidates for the nomination. In his diary for 4 September he resolved to set about this by impressing people in the area: '1st and foremost that I am a good speaker. 2ndly that I am a sound and thorough politician. 3rdly that I can afford to attend to parliamentary duties' (Morgan, 1973, p. 20). He won the nomination at a selection meeting on 20 December 1888 and was formally adopted on 3 January 1889.

In fighting the Carnarvon District constituency Lloyd George was taking on a seat which had been Liberal from 1865 until lost to Swetenham in 1886. It became marginal in the 1885 and 1886 elections, and Jones Parry's local unpopularity had a part to play in that. Before Jones Parry won it in a by-election in 1882 it had been represented since 1837 — except for the 1859 Parliament — by W. B. Hughes. He, like Gladstone, had moved from standing as a Conservative to Liberal Conservative and, from 1865, to Liberal. In selecting a local, fiery young Radical of little means, rather than a businessman or a landed gentleman, the Liberal selectors were taking a risk. Yet Lloyd George was an outstanding figure among those young activists who followed Tom Ellis rather than the more staid figures who dominated the North Wales Liberal Federation. He was also one who could be relied on to work hard in the constituency before the next General Election.

Lloyd George did campaign vigorously during the period before Swetenham's sudden death in March 1890. In those years he frequently observed that marginal seats would be won not by 'humdrum Liberalism' but by a Radicalism which would shake people out of habits of deference to well-to-do Tories. He expressed this view succinctly in the peroration of a speech he gave soon after being elected to Parliament. In it he condemned Toryism's mode of appealing to the people as coaxing them 'with promises of an occasional blanket or a quantity of coal', whereas, he said, 'Liberalism . . . raised a man

15

from the ditch and enabled him to face the highest in the land and to demand what was right for his labour' (*North Wales Observer*, 14 November 1890). It was in this spirit that he had asked Ellis in May 1887, 'Do you not think that this tithe business is an excellent lever wherewith to raise the spirit of the people?' (Morgan, 1963b, p. 86).

In attacking the landed interest, Lloyd George did so in class terms which alarmed the old guard of North Wales Liberalism. For example, in February 1890 he bluntly declared, 'Every squire fought for his property, for his castle and his class' (*Carnarvon Herald*, 15 February 1890). He also alienated the older generation of North Wales Liberals by the vigour with which he advocated Home Rule for Wales and by his public condemnations of them for being lukewarm on the issue. In calling for the fusion of the two Welsh Liberal Federations he argued that that would 'impregnate the timid genteel Liberalism of the Northern Committee with the robust, plucky Liberalism of the South' (*Carnarvon Herald*, 18 October 1889). Not surprisingly, this gave considerable offence. When Swetenham died in March 1890, A. C. Humphreys-Owen, a leading figure in the North Wales Liberal Federation, wrote to Stuart Rendel, its president:

> Lloyd George or at any rate his friends will be on their knees to us to help them − for the Boroughs can only be won by bringing Liberals who abstained in 1886 up to the poll.
>
> It would be disloyal to the party to refuse to help, but I should be glad if it were possible to get in return for it some pledges for a cessation of the vilification with which George and those who act with him have persistently employed against the Federation.   (Rendel Papers, 14/533)

Lloyd George's own instinct for self-preservation ensured that he toned down his political platform for the by-election. In his election address and in his speeches he put more emphasis on Welsh disestablishment than on any other issue. He also devoted much time to pledging himself to some moderate measures of land reform and to temperance reform. Ireland figured prominently in his election address, but while he proclaimed himself 'a firm believer in and admirer of Mr Gladstone's noble alternative of Justice to Ireland' he avoided using the word 'Home Rule' at all − neither for Ireland nor for Wales. He did state, however, that he recognized 'that the wrongs of Ireland must of necessity have the first claim upon the attention of the Liberal Party'. Not surprisingly, some Liberal activists were disgruntled at his moderation in the by-election. One wrote to him:

16

You have been bidding for the last two or three years for political popularity by dangling before the constituency Home Rule for Wales and nationalisation of the land ... I presume you have quietly dropped them to conciliate the 'moderates' whom you have always denounced. (George, 1976, pp. 168–9)

In preparing for the expected General Election contest, Lloyd George and his brother had already begun careful work on the electoral registers. Soon after being adopted he had warned his supporters, 'The aristocracy could depend upon its influence, rank, social position and the influence of capital, while in order to counteract these democracy must organise' (*Carnarvon Herald*, 15 February 1889). In April 1889 he wrote to Francis Schnadhorst, the Secretary of the National Liberal Federation, for advice on how to overcome 'the poor organisation and apathy' which he deemed responsible for the loss of the seat in 1886. As his nephew William George observed, such organizational work as they carried out before the surprise of an early by-election contest must have been crucial in giving Lloyd George victory by a mere 18 votes on 11 April 1890 (George, 1976, pp. 161–2).

This result has been depicted as a great triumph. Any by-election gain deserves to be treated as such. But the narrowness of the gain at that time does suggest that Lloyd George's parliamentary career got off to a precarious start. He might have been expected to do better, given the strength of support for Liberalism in Wales at that period. Just over a year earlier the Liberals had swept into control of all but one of the new county councils in Wales. In Carnarvonshire the Liberals had won 30 to the Conservatives' 14 seats (and subsequently had elected Lloyd George as alderman, a post to which he was re-elected for the rest of his life). Given the variable nature of electorates before universal male suffrage in 1918, comparisons between seats in by-elections has less force than in later years. But for what it is worth, Lloyd George's victory involved a swing to the Liberals of only 2 per cent, whereas a month earlier they had won St Pancras on a $4\frac{1}{4}$ per cent swing and in October were to win Eccles on just under a 3 per cent swing. Only with the 1900 General Election, when he had a 296 majority at an unfavourable time, can Lloyd George have felt reasonably confident that he had long-term prospects of keeping this seat. For him, holding his parliamentary seat was to be a major political consideration throughout the 1890s.

17

In his early years in Parliament he was an assiduous House of Commons man. As a young man, separated from his wife and family in North Wales and with little spare money, he spent long hours in the Commons and frequently raised local issues there. He clearly relished seeing such political heroes as Gladstone, Chamberlain and Parnell. He threw himself into political tussles, vying with Sam Evans, newly arrived from an uncontested by-election for Mid-Glamorgan, for recognition as the ablest, after Tom Ellis, of the young Welsh MPs. Between January and March 1891 he and Evans made their mark by waging a vigorous back-bench campaign against the Conservative Government's Tithe Bill. They also fought hard over the content of an Elementary Education Bill.

After winning much publicity for Wales (and themselves) by their activities on these Bills they went on in the autumn of 1891 to harass the Government in its efforts to pass swiftly the Clergy Discipline Bill. It was a measure which would enable the Established Church to remove clergymen found guilty of some crime or immorality. Lloyd George used it as an opportunity to attack the Established Church again. He told the Commons, 'I do not regard it as part of the functions of Parliament to attend to spiritual matters' (2, *H. C. Deb.*, 4s, 1593—1601, 31 March 1891). This was a point of view shared by some High Churchmen; but not by Gladstone, who personally came down to the Commons to hear Lloyd George and to express his displeasure. Lloyd George revelled in putting Welsh obstruction again at the forefront of Westminster politics, and proudly reported to his wife one MP's view that they had fought their battle 'much more skilfully than the Irishmen used to do' (Morgan, 1973, p. 52).

That Lloyd George had disregarded his venerable leader dismayed some Liberals in Carnarvon District and was used against him by the Conservatives in the 1892 General Election. Humphreys-Owen commented to Rendel, 'George is fighting a desperate game', but added, 'The Welsh are to be flattered by any appeal to Welsh fire and Welsh enthusiasm and the like, that such a course will appeal strongly to them' (Owen to Rendel, 26 May 1892; Rendel Papers 14, 617). In all probability Lloyd George's bold efforts to highlight Welsh issues did go down well among his constituents. Both he and Evans received many congratulations on their stand. In one letter Evans was told: 'Glad you are not going to follow the G.O.M. blindly. As a nonconformist I never had too much respect for Mr Gladstone, and his conduct lately tends to make it less' (J. M. Prydderch to Evans, 26 May, 1892; S. T. Evans Papers 43).

During the 1890s Lloyd George continued to campaign for Welsh disestablishment. He spoke at the inauguration of a new Welsh disestablishment campaign on 10 September 1891 and at a series of meetings in subsequent months. In the 1892 General Election, as in the 1890 by-election, he put the issue to the forefront of his programme. Earlier, speaking in Manchester he had declared:

It was the question of Disestablishment that had brought Wales to the feet of the Liberal Party, and, although they had inculcated many noble principles since, they had not forgotten their first love. They placed the great principle of religious equality and freedom first and foremost in their political creed. (*Carnarvon Herald*, 7 November 1890)

This was an early warning that Lloyd George would put achievement of this Welsh goal before 'blind support' of the Liberal Party leadership.

The narrow victory of the Liberal Party in the 1892 General Election put the ball in Lloyd George's court. His parliamentary guerrilla tactics had raised expectations. Before the election one prominent activist had told Humphreys-Owen that Lloyd George and 'the rest of the irreconcilables have done good work' in showing 'people in London that Wales is in earnest'. He added, 'If we don't fight, Welsh questions will be postponed by one great English question after another and nothing ever will be done in our generation' (Humphreys-Owen to Rendel, 27 May, 1895; Rendel Papers 14, 618). For the Welsh Liberal Parliamentary Party, with its 31 MPs at a time when the government's majority – including the Irish Nationalists – was only 40, it was then or never to try the tactic of insisting on disestablishment as the price of its support for other measures. Rendel and others pointed out that all manner of groups within the Liberal majority could make similar claims, and that, if they all did so, the Liberals' ability to govern would be destroyed. But for Lloyd George, with a majority of still only 196 in his constituency and a commitment to achieving disestablishment quickly, there were limits to his patience.

Soon after Gladstone's new government was formed in July 1892 Tom Ellis, now a Government Whip, reassured Lloyd George that Sir William Harcourt (Chancellor of the Exchequer and Gladstone's second-in-command in the Commons) had told him that 'they mean business' with regard to Welsh disestablishment and two other measures. The following summer Lloyd George was still willing to work with Ellis, Rendel and the Welsh Parliamentary Party rather

19

than support the plans of D. A. Thomas, MP for Merthyr Tydfil, for an independent Welsh Party. However, Lloyd George's restraint went with Gladstone's resignation on 3 March 1894 and Rendel's elevation to the peerage. On the day of Gladstone's resignation he wrote to his brother that the only part he would have in the new political situation would be 'to try and extract terms out of the incoming Prime Minister on Welsh Disestablishment' (George, 1983, pp. 101, 121–2, 141). After Harcourt, now Leader of the House of Commons as well as Chancellor of the Exchequer, had bluntly declined to give Welsh disestablishment priority in the Government's programme, Thomas, Lloyd George, Frank Edwards and, a few days later, Herbert Lewis announced that they would no longer accept the Liberal Whip.

Lloyd George explained his position to a meeting of constituents in the Carnarvon Reform Club on 14 April 1894. He deplored how Welsh disestablishment, which had held second place in the Newcastle Programme of the Liberal Party, had slipped to 'tail-end' in the Queen's Speech. He declared, 'I have paired for the Budget and Registration Bill, but, as for voting on anything else, I will not, whatever may be the consequence.' He added, with a little of the rancour which was often apparent in his speeches of this period, 'It is a Cabinet of Churchmen. There are some who were originally Nonconformist, but they left their Nonconformity behind immediately they came in contact with the atmosphere of London society' (*North Wales Observer*, 20 April 1894).

In his revolt Lloyd George drew explicit parallels with the Irish Parliamentary Party. He toyed with becoming the Parnell of Wales. With no more of his Welsh parliamentary colleagues joining him, Lloyd George turned to the constituencies to try to build on the nationalist enthusiasm which was aroused in some quarters by the 'Revolt of the Four'. By late May 1894 Lloyd George was speaking of federating the existing *Cymru Fydd* ('Wales to Be') societies as a vehicle for Welsh nationalism. On 22 and 23 August a *Cymru Fydd* League was launched at Llandrindod Wells. Lloyd George was soon making passionate nationalist speeches on its behalf throughout Wales. At its formal inaugural meeting in Cardiff on 11 October 1894 he reiterated the nationalist theme he had been developing during 'the revolt':

Immediately it is made manifest at by-elections, mass meetings or otherwise that England has made up her mind definitely that she wants anything, it matters not what Party is in power, the

20

demands of the predominant partner are attended to. ... The main factor in British legislation is therefore not so much which Ministry is in office as is what is required by England at the hands of the Ministry. If anyone suffers ... it is the Celtic nationalities of this kingdom.

He went on to dwell on the success of the Irish nationalists (*Carnarvon Herald*, 12 October 1894).

In the House of Commons H. H. Asquith, the Home Secretary, introduced a radical measure of Welsh disestablishment a fortnight after Lloyd George and his associates announced their revolt. As Rosebery, Gladstone's successor as Prime Minister, would offer no guarantee of early government time for the Bill to pass through the Commons the 'Four' remained formally in revolt. By the time the Government arranged for a revised Welsh Disestablishment Bill to pass through Committee stage in the House of Commons in May and June 1895 the Government was in terminal decline. Lloyd George, by manoeuvring to tack on to the Bill the setting up of a Welsh National Council (a step towards devolution), became one of several contributors to its demise. Asquith afterwards bitterly complained of 'the underhand and disloyal way in which he undoubtedly acted' (Morgan, 1963b, pp. 152–8). As was so often the case when his actions ended badly, Lloyd George loudly proclaimed his innocence as if he were the aggrieved party. He did this well enough to prevent doubts growing widely about his role until after the General Election, in which he was remarkably successful in holding his seat with his majority cut by only two votes (to 194) at a time when the Liberal Party in general did badly.

Lloyd George undoubtedly risked his political career during the 'Revolt of the Four'. In an interview in the autumn of 1894 he said that if he lost his seat it would not be too dreadful, for parliamentary life was not that pleasant (*Carnarvon Herald*, 26 October 1894). He risked all, but he played to win both political leadership in Wales and also the legislation he saw as Wales's just desert. In 1892 a Welsh newspaperman commenting on Welsh disestablishment told Sam Evans, 'now Lloyd George has stolen it from you and ... he will become the next Welsh leader' (H. Evans to S. T. Evans, 25 February 1892; S. T. Evans Papers 18).

Lloyd George's leadership ambitions soon led to friction with D. A. Thomas. Thomas had promoted Welsh national issues earlier than Lloyd George. In January 1892 Lloyd George had travelled to Thomas's constituency and spoken in support of Thomas's National

Institutions Bill. In 1893, after the formation of a Liberal Government, Thomas had taken the lead in pressing for an independent line and he may also have taken the lead in the actual revolt of April 1894. So in 1895, while Lloyd George and his *Cymru Fydd* movement were in the ascendant in North Wales Liberalism, Thomas helped to ensure that South Wales Liberalism thwarted Lloyd George's plans for a united Welsh Liberal Federation. A stormy meeting at Newport on 16 January 1896 ended Lloyd George's aspirations to be a Welsh Parnell, and soon afterwards the *Cymru Fydd* movement collapsed.

During the 'Revolt of the Four' Lloyd George became contemptuous of those of his Welsh parliamentary colleagues who failed to rebel. In a letter to his wife in May 1894 he dubbed them 'cowards who would not even criticise our action in our presence when we challenged them but who condemn us when our backs are turned' (Morgan, 1973, p. 72). He had also aroused distrust as well as animosity. From 1896 Lloyd George moved towards all parliamentary Radicals, and away from being enmeshed in purely Welsh concerns within the Welsh Parliamentary Party. In 1897 when Osborne Morgan died, Lloyd George either declined or failed to go for the Welsh Parliamentary Party's vacant leadership. This may have been because he was threatened at that time with a paternity suit which could have ruined his political career (but of which he was cleared in November). Most likely, he was no longer interested.

By March 1901 Humphreys-Owen was writing to Rendel:

> The Welsh Party does not exist. It committed suicide when it put that worthy old pantaloon Alfred Thomas into the Chair. We made an irreparable blunder in not taking Lloyd George. We were cowards. We ought to have felt that if we made him our leader we should be able to keep him in order, but partly through honest mistrust of his judgement and partly through jealousy of some of his competitors we refused him.

Humphreys-Owen went on to report, 'George is now fighting for his own hand and is a below the gangway English Radical — nothing more — and is doing that admirably' (Rendel Papers, 14, 689a).

After the collapse of the *Cymru Fydd* movement Lloyd George continued to build on his nonconformist support, both in Wales and outside. This was to be crucial to his leading role in the opposition to Balfour's Education Act of 1902. But from 1896 the emphasis in his role as a Welsh nonconformist politician was increasingly on the nonconformist rather than nationalist aspect. Yet it would be wrong to understate his often close interest in Welsh political developments up to, and even after, the First World War. Sir Maurice Hankey, the Cabinet Secretary, noted in his diary on 31 December 1918 when staying with Lloyd George at Criccieth, 'Many drives about the constituency interlanded with speeches in Welsh, cheers and interminable conversations about local Welsh politics' (Hankey Papers, HNKY 1/5, f.65). Of course, from about 1902 onwards, as the pre-eminent Welsh figure in national politics, Welsh matters naturally gravitated his way.

Lloyd George remained supportive of, even if no longer fervent for, the cause of Welsh disestablishment and saw that cause to a successful conclusion. After the Liberals' 1906 General Election victory he appears to have been willing to arrange a compromise disestablishment measure through informal discussions with the Bishop of St Asaph. However, nothing came of his offer to the Anglicans of 'a very mild and kindly Welsh Disestablishment Bill' (Purvey-Tyrer, 1991, pp. 153–5). The issue was put off until 1909 by means of a Royal Commission, when Asquith (who had moved Bills in 1894 and 1895) introduced a Welsh Church Bill. This, however, fell with the political crisis over the 1909 Budget.

Lloyd George still needed to be seen to be working for disestablishment. When Ellis Griffiths was appointed Under-Secretary at the Home Office in early 1912 to help prepare a Disestablishment Bill, Lloyd George wrote to him wishing him success and professing his old faith in the justice of such a measure. In declamatory style, Lloyd George observed:

Surely a nation is entitled to a determining voice in the settlement of its own national religion. To insist on treating a faith which the Welsh people do not accept as if it were their national creed; to continue forcing it upon them as such, in spite of their repeated repudiation of the claim; to divert compulsorily the whole of the ancient national endowment to its maintenance, is the most intolerable of all oppressions. (Lloyd George to Griffiths, 25 January 1912; Ellis Griffiths Papers, 449)

Lloyd George intervened in the House of Commons debates on the Bill, exercising his wit on aristocratic opponents of disestablishment. After rejection by the Lords, the Bill passed twice more through the Commons before being suspended, like the Irish Home Rule Bill, soon after the outbreak of war in 1914 (Morgan, 1963b, pp. 260–73).

23

After the First World War, Lloyd George again intervened both in private negotiations and in Commons debates to ensure that the detailed arrangements which had been worked out during the war were still carried through. His old colleague and friend Herbert Lewis noted in his diary on 22 July 1919:

> The Conservative Party have a majority in the House of Commons and but for the Prime Minister they would have repealed the Welsh Disestablishment Act by a Bill of a single line. And it is only the power and glamour of his personality which enabled him to carry through this settlement. (J. H. Lewis Papers 10/231/130)

While it is often rightly commented that the formal disestablishment of the Welsh Church on 31 March 1920 was a matter which by then aroused little public interest even in Wales, credit is given less often to Lloyd George for using his political power to ensure that a policy he had long advocated did come to fruition.

# 3

## From Old-Style Radical to New Liberal

Between 1908 and 1911 Lloyd George emerged as a dynamic force behind the most imaginative of the Liberal Government's social reforms. In these years Lloyd George saw both the need and the opportunity to do something for the unorganized working class – those downtrodden members of society who were aided neither by inherited wealth nor by a strong bargaining position within the labour market. This role was all the more remarkable given that Lloyd George had been an outstanding champion of the older Radical causes linked with nonconformity and had previously shown relatively little interest in social welfare measures.

After the defeat of the Liberals in the 1895 General Election Lloyd George looked to the Radicals in Parliament to give a lead in regenerating the Liberal Party. His involvement in efforts to form 'a distinctive Radical section in Parliament, and to appeal to the Radical element in the Liberal Party and in the constituencies to carry on an active and energetic campaign' (to quote from a manifesto which he signed) appears a natural sequel to his earlier efforts to turn the Welsh Liberal MPs into a powerful pressure group within the Liberal Party. In this attempt to form a pressure group of Radical MPs Lloyd George worked with the older generation such as Sir Charles Dilke and Henry Labouchere as well as with younger MPs representing Welsh seats, such as Sam Evans and Reginald McKenna (Lucy, 1905, pp. 428–30). Little came of this attempt. When in early 1903 Keir Hardie appealed to Lloyd George, John Morley or John Burns 'to lead a Progressive Alliance of Radicals, Irish and Labour with the battle-cry of "People versus Privilege"', Lloyd George had by this time graduated beyond pressure groups within the Parliamentary Liberal Party to being a power within the party of sufficient standing to be among those consulted by the party Leader.

Lloyd George's progress to the forefront of Liberal politics was marked by hard work in the House of Commons and on Liberal and nonconformist platforms across the country; by seizing several opportunities to project himself as the spokesperson of British, not just Welsh, nonconformity; and by considerable manoeuvring around the leadership figures of Sir William Harcourt, Sir Henry Campbell-Bannerman and Lord Rosebery in the years 1898–1905. In 1896 Lloyd George was very much a politician looking for a cause to ignite his political career – or at least a parliamentary opportunity. Herbert Lewis recalled Lloyd George saying in early 1896 that to build his reputation he intended to rely not on set-piece speeches in the House of Commons but rather 'to go in for the rough-and-tumble-day-by-day-fighting' (J. H. Lewis Papers, 10.231/4).

In this way Lloyd George was ready to seize his opportunity when, in the spring of 1896, Lord Salisbury's Government introduced an Agricultural Land Rating Bill. As J. Hugh Edwards later commented, 'by a happy stroke of fortune [he] had served his articles as a solicitor in an office where agricultural rating constituted the staple interest. In this way he had been able to grasp the question in all its intricate bearings' (Souvenir Programme marking the presentation of the Freedom of Cardiff to Lloyd George, 1908). Lloyd George, reminiscing in early 1920, remembered it as the issue which had made his reputation in the House of Commons:

> Knowledge is what tells ... I happened to know a good deal about it and Charles Harrison, another solicitor member [for Plymouth], was also well versed in the subject but he was a poor speaker and was always getting ruled out of order. So he gave me his stuff. Added to my own it enabled me to make a very strong statement. (Diary, 1 January 1920; see Riddell, 1933b, p. 158)

Lloyd George made strong attacks on landlords, including a personal one on Henry Chaplin who, as President of the Local Government Board, was the minister responsible for the Agricultural Land Rating Bill. He deemed Chaplin likely to benefit by £700 per annum if it became law. More generally, Lloyd George made the charge that 'the real purpose of the measure was not to relieve agricultural distress, but to unfairly relieve one class of property – agricultural land – of half the rates at the expense of the rest of the community'. In his criticisms he was careful to align himself with the farmers, suggesting that rate relief was a very ineffective way of helping those who bore the brunt of the agricultural depression. Thus he observed of the landlords, 'They were not suffering in the actual and real sense of the word, the same as the farmers who had got their sons working hard like labourers on a farm and who yet were receiving no wages' (House of Commons, 30 April, 18 and 20 May 1896; 40 and 41 *H. C. Deb.*, 4s, cols 237–40, 1638, 38).

Lloyd George pushed his opposition to the Bill so far that he was suspended from the House of Commons on 21 May 1896 for refusing to obey the Speaker when he tried to put part of the Bill to the vote. Herbert Lewis, who had supported him throughout his long-running obstruction of the passage of the Bill, was also suspended, as were Michael Davitt, John Dillon and three other Irish MPs during the ensuing uproar. This incident not only provides a late example of Lloyd George playing the part of a Welsh martyr, but is also a fairly common example (at this time) of his appealing to fellow Celts, be they Scots or Irish. It was as well the first instance in which he is seen savouring the role of parliamentary leader of the Liberal Party as a whole. While Sir William Harcourt could not support such insubordination to the Speaker, he did applaud Lloyd George's more orthodox activities in opposing the Bill and paid tribute to these in a speech in the Commons. Harcourt himself vigorously condemned the Bill as having 'its origins in the same spirit as inspired the Corn Laws' (Gardiner, 1923, pp. 405–6).

This success just added further fuel to his striking determination to make his mark at the forefront of Liberal politics. The problem was to find further strong issues. In September 1897 he wrote to his wife that H. W. Massingham, editor of the *Daily Chronicle* (a Liberal newspaper):

> is anxious I should take in hand the resurrecting of the Liberal Party and do what Lord Randolph Churchill did for the Tory party. He says that I am the man to do it and he'll back me through thick and thin. I told him I would do it provided we could agree on a definite line of policy.  (Letter of 9 September 1897, in Morgan, 1973, p. 112)

The following August, he commented to his wife, 'Whether I am offered a seat in the next Liberal Cabinet or not ... it is not without satisfaction to feel that a great number of keen, intelligent politicians assume that I must needs be in' (letter of 30 August 1898, in Morgan, 1973, 115). This was notable confidence in a politician still only 35 years old.

The way in which he moved forward was by building on and broadening out from his Welsh nonconformist causes in order to try to serve the political leadership of Liberal-inclined British nonconformity. This was a natural development, given the prominence of Welsh disestablishment in the Liberal Party programme and the recognition among disestablishers that Welsh disestablishment was politically more feasible than Scottish or English. Lloyd George had in any case been quick to take up other causes dear to nonconformity – such as temperance or educational matters – from the time he had entered Parliament.

Nonconformity in Britain in the 1890s was self-confident and politically assertive. There was greater interdenominational co-ordination with the spread of the Evangelical Free Church Council movement, which was marked by annual national congresses from 1892, the establishment of a National Council in 1896 and the creation of a Nonconformist Parliamentary Council in 1898 to press Parliament to take note of issues of special concern to dissenters. In Parliament itself the number of MPs who were nonconformists jumped from 95 in 1886 to 177 in 1892 (though the members were to drop back in the poor Liberal results of the 1895 and 1900 General Elections). In the country as a whole the number of nonconformists did not fall until about 1906, even if they did not keep pace with the growth of the population and so fell as a proportion of the population from the mid-1880s (Koss, 1975, p. 28; Machin, 1987, pp. 206–7, 221–2).

Lloyd George linked himself with the major nonconformist organizations and newspapers. For example, he served on the committee of the Liberation Society, which between 1844 and 1958 was the main pressure group for disestablishment. Though he attended its committee meetings irregularly, nevertheless on at least two occasions in the mid-1890s he pushed the Society into activities which embarrassed staider Liberals. With the struggle against Balfour's 1902 Education Act, Lloyd George became one of the Society's vice-presidents (Bebbington, 1982, pp. 23–4, 35). As for the Nonconformist Parliamentary Council, Lloyd George moved the motion on 24 May 1898 which set it up. This complained of 'recent reactionary legislation seriously affecting the interests of Nonconformists and the efforts now being made by organisations connected with the Anglican and Roman Catholic Churches to carry the nation further in the same direction', and urged that the Council should be formed 'to examine and watch measures submitted to Parliament, to assist in forming a strong Nonconformist opinion on political issues of moment to the Free Churches, to communicate with the public departments on such questions, and to promote by every means in its power effective legislation for the removal of the grievances now admittedly suffered by Nonconformists' (*Daily News*, 25 May 1898).

As had been the case with Welsh nationalist issues, Lloyd George was strong in backing some of the most advanced (or extreme) aspects of the interest he was furthering. This was so during the anti-ritual controversies of 1895 to 1905, during which John Kensit and his 'Wycliffe preachers' harassed Anglican clergymen who were deemed to be ritualists, and when books such as *England's Danger* (1898) by R. F. Horton warned of 'Romanism', much as a decade later alarmist writers warned of the German menace (Machin, 1987, pp. 234–55). In making much of ritualism he joined the then Liberal leader Sir William Harcourt. Thus at a meeting of the Baptist Union in Birmingham on 29 September 1898 Lloyd George warned that 'they were face to face with the most resolute, pertinacious and best organised attempt to re-establish the power of the priesthood in this country since the days of the Reformation' (*Birmingham Daily Express*, 30 September 1898). While his repeated invocations of Cromwell, Hampden and Gladstone were norms of nonconformist oratory, appeals such as that at a Free Church rally – 'Should England, the refuge of the slave, the land of Wycliffe and Oliver Cromwell, put on now the manacles of the priest?' – had added connotations in the decade of anti-ritualist demonstrations (*Daily News*, 13 July 1903).

Although discrediting the Protestantism of part of the established Church helped the cause of Welsh disestablishment, such utterances by Lloyd George and others hardly fostered relations between the Liberals and the Irish Nationalists. Indeed in 1898, when he opposed an Irish Nationalist amendment calling for state funding for a Catholic university, he banged the Protestant drum while calling for secular education:

We think we ought to protest against the idea that Protestantism is a kind of leprosy from which the Catholic youth of Ireland should be protected. The Irish people have no right to come to a Protestant nation and ask them to vote funds for the purpose of setting up a university based on the assumption that Protestantism is a contagion from which Catholics must be saved. (Quoted in George, 1983, p. 264)

Though Lloyd George was to be close to some of the Irish MPs over the Boer War, he appears not to have been too distraught at nonconformist pressure to downgrade the priority of Irish Home Rule in favour of upgrading other issues. It may well be that Lloyd George himself – as Adams later felt (see p. 14) – had a certain latent hostility to Catholicism within him.

This may *in part* explain Lloyd George's somewhat surprising political flirtations with Lord Rosebery at various times in the decade after 1895; surprising given Rosebery's position as the leading Liberal Imperialist. Rosebery had some significant nonconformist support for his policy of dumping the Liberal commitment to Home Rule, and he and his supporters sought to foster such support, not least when in 1899 he paid for the statue of Cromwell which stands beside the Houses of Parliament (Koss, 1975, pp. 30–4). Lloyd George may have hoped that Rosebery would take up his preferred solution, Home Rule All Round, as well as social reform.

Lloyd George was also vigorous in pushing the Liberation Society's viewpoint on education. Many nonconformists were vehemently against state funding of denominational schools. They had been angered when Gladstone's first Government had included in its 1870 Education Act a clause which allowed the continued subsidy of voluntary schools. When Salisbury's Government in 1891 introduced a Bill to enable elementary schools to provide free education, Lloyd George took up the line of the Liberation Society and its offshoot, the National Education Association, that denominational schools should only receive rate aid if under popular control. In urging popular control in the Commons on 23 June 1891 he declared, 'I protest against a Bill which is nothing more or less than the further endowment of the Church of England in Wales, which is already too highly endowed' (354 *H. C. Deb. 4s*, 1301). However, opposing free elementary education on the grounds of lack of popular control was hardly a political winner, as Lord Salisbury had shrewdly judged when the bill was designed (Bebbington, 1982, pp. 133–4).

In 1896, when Salisbury's government rashly introduced an Education Bill which included increased state aid to voluntary schools and relieved them of paying rates, it united nonconformist opposition and divided the Government's own supporters (Machin, 1987, pp. 226–30). In a series of speeches round Wales that year Lloyd George made much of the proposal that church schools would be funded by a few shillings per pupil whereas nonconformist schools would receive nothing. The Government withdrew its Bill and instead

30

brought in a simpler measure in early 1897, the Voluntary Schools Bill, which again offered these schools financial assistance, this time five shillings (25p) per pupil. But the Government undercut much of the opposition by promising, and then introducing, a Necessitous Board Schools Bill to provide some funding for nonconformist schools.

Harcourt invited Lloyd George to help lead the Liberal opposition to the Voluntary Schools Bill in the Commons (George, 1983, p. 261). In so doing Lloyd George again vigorously condemned Anglican proselytizing through schools and called for popular representation in school management (46 *H. C. Deb. 4s*, 465–71 and 1156–62; 15 and 25 February 1897). Where Lloyd George excelled in his opposition to the measure was not in the freshness of his arguments but, as the journalist Henry Lucy commented at the time, by the 'sheer ability' with which he successfully mastered the procedures of the House of Commons (Grigg, 1973, p. 213).

He was perfectly placed to take up the nonconformist cudgels in 1902 when Balfour, on behalf of Salisbury's Government, introduced another Education Bill. This proposed the creation of new education authorities: county or large borough councils which would take over responsibility for secondary education and would have the option of taking over denominational or nonconformist elementary schools. Lloyd George was particularly critical of the optional element in it (which was removed during the passage of the Bill) and, like most nonconformists, was opposed to funds from the rates going to the voluntary schools without full public control and while school authorities were still able to maintain religious tests in the appointment of head teachers. However Lloyd George had at first been attracted by the Bill's provision for local authority control of the schools. In all this he was consistent. He had often enunciated two great principles for education. First was 'that of public control over denominational schools', which he justified at a Welsh Baptist Conference by arguing, 'If the denominational schools were controlled by the parents it would be absolutely impossible for the priests to use them as kinds of nurseries for proselytism.' His second principle was 'local self-government in educational matters', which in most of Wales would put the nonconformists in a very strong position (*Carnarvon Herald*, 4 October 1895). Thus Balfour's Bill was for him a mixture of good and bad. John Grigg has deemed his part in the controversy to be an 'important rather than a glorious episode' in his career because his line 'was largely insincere' (Grigg, 1978, p. 49). This is too harsh a judgement. Undoubtedly he availed himself of a golden political opportunity, but in so doing he was only developing arguments he had long been making.

Balfour's proposals succeeded in dividing the Irish Nationalists from the nonconformists, as the former supported the Bill because it gave rate aid to Catholic as well as to Anglican schools. But the Bill soon united nearly all nonconformists in opposition to it. Lloyd George again was not backward in banging the Protestant drum. Thus at Criccieth on 12 May 1902 he asked his audience how they accounted for a vote in the Commons on the Bill where 'the Irish members almost as a body had voted in its favour whilst some Conservatives voted against it'. He provided the answer:

> The Irishmen and the few Conservatives saw into the future. They saw the Education Bill indirectly steering the country back to Roman Catholicism. The few Conservatives whom he had mentioned were staunch Protestants and wished to save their country if they could. (*Carnarvon Herald*, 16 May 1902)

With speeches such as that, with renewed invocations of Cromwell, Hampden and the like, little wonder that four months later, on 17 September, he could tell an audience at Bangor that 'the Protestants of the North of Ireland, who were against him on Home Rule and the war question, had written to him to say that Ulster was agreed against the measure' (*Carnarvon Herald*, 19 September 1902).

Yet Lloyd George also made more positive comments on the need for educational reform. In this he was much influenced by Rosebery, whom he was then publicly praising (Gilbert, 1987, p. 223). In December 1902, speaking at an Eastern Counties Liberal Federation meeting, he gave a speech in which he urged that better education was necessary for the industrial and agricultural efficiency of Britain as well as being good because it 'increases the power, widens the range and improves the quality of the pleasures of life'. In the speech he urged the need for better education 'as we are engaged in a series of wars more dangerous to our supremacy than the South African war. ... An industrial war, a war for commercial supremacy.' He went on:

> We ought to train our men. On the continent, they train every man in the use of arms. We ought to train every man in the use of his industrial arms ... unless we are trained we will be beaten by better trained countries.

He also urged better education as a means of ending the class war:

> Capital might get a better remuneration without reducing wages. Wages might be increased, and still get better returns for capital. Above all, the improved conditions of labour would bring the end of civil war between capital and labour, which destroys industry and creates bitterness and strife. (*Lincoln Leader*, 13 December 1902)

Thus he argued on both a higher and a lower plane.

After the Education Bill because law in December 1902 Lloyd George took the lead in organizing resistance to it in Wales. At a Welsh National Liberal meeting held in Cardiff on 20 January 1903 he urged that opposition to the Act should stay within the law, otherwise 'each party would decline to obey an Act carried by its opponents', and deplored the example set by the Unionist leaders in 1893 over Ulster. His plan, outlined in his *Address to the People of Wales* of 17 January 1903, relied on the mostly nonconformist-dominated Welsh county councils not operating the Act under various pretexts unless they gained concessions. He urged the councils to withhold rate aid unless there were public control of the schools and the schools gave up imposing religious tests when appointing teachers. 'No Control, No Cash!', as he put it in the *Address* (*South Wales Daily News*, 21 January 1903; Du Parq, 1912–13, pp. 412–16)

However, for all his public fervour on the issue, Lloyd George was willing to try to reach a compromise. In February and March 1903 he attempted to reach an accommodation with an old adversary in religious matters, the Bishop of St Asaph. While the Bishop and Lloyd George could reach agreement on many issues, the Bishop's diocese and fellow Welsh bishops were unwilling to follow his lead. Of these negotiations Professor Morgan has commented, 'it is remarkable how much agreement was reached, including an acceptance of the syllabus of religious instruction given by the London School Board' (Morgan, 1963b, p. 189); while Professor Gilbert has pointed to the stenographer's record of the last of these negotiations, on 24 March 1903, as:

> the first verbatim textual example of the negotiating technique that Lloyd George would make famous in later years. He would pretend to misunderstand questions, assert that he was speaking only for himself or assume the power to commit the county councils as circumstances warranted, contradict stands he had taken publicly, when as he put it, he 'had his war paint on'. (Gilbert, 1987, pp. 237–8)

33

Indeed, Lloyd George's willingness to compromise, to go to the political middle ground, had been shown as early as 1891, also over education. Then, when pressing the case for popular control of elementary education in the House of Commons, he said to his Conservative opponents:

> If these grievances are removed, the energies of a large number of able men, which are now devoted to the redress of these wrongs, will be set free for other objects, and thus the country will benefit. .... Every grievance redressed adds force to conservatism in the higher sense; every wrong perpetuated adds strength to the forces of the revolution. England requires the services, the energies, the enthusiasm of men now devoted to the redress of wrongs for other important national matters. You have in Wales the best men on either side – Churchmen and Nonconformists – devoting their energies to this deplorable struggle, and meantime you have the population reduced to such a condition that on 1 January, one person in every 19 of the population was in receipt of parish relief. We want, I say, the energies of our people devoted to raising the social conditions of the nation.   (354 *H. C. Deb. 3s*, 1315; 24 June 1891)

The habit of mind behind Lloyd George's willingness to take off his 'war paint' even at the height of political conflict, which he displayed in 1903 and 1910, went back a long way.

However in 1903, as in 1910, no deal could be concluded. And so Lloyd George advised that the 'Welsh revolt' should go ahead. His strategy of getting the county councils to not implement the Act proved popular in Wales and in the short term effective in disrupting the legislation. In February 1904 supporters of this policy swept to victory in the Welsh county council elections, even in Brecon and Radnor which previously had had Unionist majorities. Lloyd George emerged as very much the key figure in Welsh politics – and had provided a boost to the morale of both Liberal-inclined British nonconformity and the Liberal Party as a whole.

While the Boer War made Lloyd George a national figure, his role in opposing the 1902 Education Act transformed him from a promising figure for a ministerial post into a near-certainty for Cabinet office. The education issue electrified much of British nonconformity and provided Lloyd George with a platform for which both his personal and his wider Welsh background fully equipped him to take a lead. Moreover, his dynamism contrasted with the pallid performances of surviving ministers of the Gladstone and Rosebery governments. As in 1897, he also excelled in his parliamentary performance. The Liberal journalist H. W. Massingham wrote in the *Daily News*, 'Save Gladstone, I recall no Committee debater so good as Mr George' (Cregier, 1976, p. 79). Balfour paid him the compliment in the Commons of describing the conduct of his opposition to the Bill there as being 'most distinguished', showing him 'to be an eminent Parliamentarian'.

Balfour's government also presented him in 1904 with another issue which was capable of arousing most nonconformists – a Licensing Bill, though this was of much lesser political weight as a controversy than the 1902 Education Bill. The Licensing Bill proposed to give publicans compensation for any licenses that were revoked for reasons other than misconduct. This enraged temperance supporters as it formally made licences a valuable form of private property. At a meeting in his constituency at Bangor on 30 April 1904 he pledged, 'I will oppose ... any Bill which will raise up a barrier almost insuperable, a wall, an impregnable rampart, around the worst and most dangerous enemy that ever menaced this Empire' (*North Wales Observer*, 6 May 1904).

Again, Lloyd George was a consistent denouncer of the evils of drink, though his approach became less narrow as time went by. In 1890 he had taken the extreme line that 'temperance reform must precede all other social reforms'. At that time Lloyd George was an active and important advocate for the United Kingdom Alliance within the Liberal Party, pushing forward its policy of a direct popular veto. By 1894 he was arguing that temperance reform involved more than just closing public houses. 'Poverty, misery, the sense of wrong, ill treatment by our social system, squalor, dinginess, the lack of proper nourishment, and the environment which surrounds the poorest classes', all had to be dealt with if the evils of drink were to be conquered. In his speech at Bangor in late April 1904 he adopted the caution of one expecting soon to be in office, observing that 'the temperance question was not going to be settled by teetotallers ... legislation on temperance lines must be legislation which would appeal to men who were not total abstainers.' Yet even into the First World War he was still speaking out against drink. To the wrath of many trade union leaders, he was still giving it what they felt to be undue weight as a cause of low productivity in munitions in 1915 (Wrigley, 1976, pp. 9, 107–8, 241).

Lloyd George joined with Asquith and other leaders in proclaiming the merits of Free Trade against Tariff Reform, a cause which

Joseph Chamberlain unleashed as the major political issue in British politics in 15 May 1903. But in this Asquith took the lead. For Lloyd George, Free Trade was not the most sacred element in his political faith; but he was less equivocal about it than many historians have suggested. John Grigg was sagacious in his assessment that 'he was Cobdenite in identifying Free Trade with efficiency, prosperity and the cause of international peace. On balance, his instinct and his judgment led him to oppose Chamberlain's tariff policy' (Grigg, 1978, pp. 61–2).

Once Chamberlain raised the standard of Tariff Reform, Lloyd George was quick to understand that there was to be a serious battle of ideas which would go further than just trade policy. Over the next 11 years he tried to show that under Free Trade the Liberals could offer new measures of public finance and social reform that met the political needs of the time. His initial packages were familiar remedies. Churchill, after lunching with Lloyd George on 31 December 1903, reported to Lord Hugh Cecil:

> He wants to promise three things which are arranged to deal with three different classes, namely, fixity of tenure to tenant farmers subject to payments of rents and good husbandry; taxation of site values to reduce rates in the towns; and of course something in the nature of Shackleton's Trade Disputes Bill for the Trade Unionists. Of course with regard to brewers he would write 'no compensation out of public funds.'

Churchill added, quite accurately, 'after all Lloyd George represents three things – Wales, English Radicalism and Nonconformists, and they are not three things which politicians can overlook' (quoted in Gilbert, 1987, pp. 267–8).

The extent to which Lloyd George's social reform policies of 1908–11 were a new direction for him has been much discussed. As Bentley Gilbert has observed of the items in the programme that Lloyd George outlined to Churchill, they did not 'add up to social reform in the sense it would come to be understood. ... The programme to blunt the appeal of tariff reform was in essence land reform' (Gilbert, 1987, p. 268). Yet taking Lloyd George's pronouncements during his time as a back-bench MP (1890–1905), there are present many of the seeds which he would cultivate in 1908–11. In the case of the People's Budget (1909), Watkin Davies has argued that 'it is possible to deduce from the speeches of that period all the proposals which underlie the most famous orations of the Budget campaign' (W. W. Davies, 1939, pp. 226, 107). In this he followed Lloyd George's own argument expressed in the preface of *Better Times* (Lloyd George, 1910, p. vii), a collection of speeches.

From early in his career Lloyd George had asserted the need to redistribute wealth. Thus at Bangor on 21 May 1891 he declared, 'It is not in the creation of wealth that England lacks, but in its distribution.' He told his audience that

> the whole weight of an unproductive class like the landlord must necessarily fall upon those who work. You cannot spare large incomes to men who will not work without lowering the wages, lengthening the hours and impoverishing and oppressing those who toil for their daily bread. If you mean to get better hours, better wages, better conditions of life, you can only do so by trenching upon the enormous rent-rolls and revenues of landlords and monopolists of all descriptions. (*Carnarvon Herald*, 22 May 1891)

Such sentiments would not have been out of place at the massive first May Day demonstrations in London of 1890 and 1891. Lloyd George may well have drawn on the Progressive sentiments of that time.

On occasion he also broke away from the old Radicalism of 'Peace, Retrenchment and Reform' to suggest that reform would cost extra money. Thus, for example, at Scarborough on 17 April 1901 he was reported as saying:

> He was not one of those who said: 'You must judge a Corporation or a School Board purely by the rates levied.' They must judge the bodies by the results produced. If the rates were spent wisely on the improvement of the town, then it was a wise Corporation, even though it increased the rates. (*Scarborough Evening News*, 18 April 1701)

He was to say virtually the same thing in the 1930s (for example, in the Commons, 12 July 1932; 268 *H. C. Deb. 5s*, 1176–7). Yet equally on occasion before the 1906 General Election he was happy to repeat the old Radical litany. Thus at a Cobden Centenary rally at the Alexandra Palace on 4 June 1904 he commented 'that the only guarantees for Free Trade were peace, small armaments, reduction of the National Debt and less taxation' (*Daily News*, 6 June 1904). While this is not an unexpected observation at such an occasion it was by no means unique. His own People's Budget was to break out of this intellectual strait-jacket and to offer a Free Trade solution to financing both social reform and increased naval armaments.

Before 1906 he was also explicitly arguing the case for state intervention. Thus at Bangor in December 1896 he commented, 'state interference, after all, simply means the concentration of the power of all for the protection of each.' He also observed:

> Formerly all parties alike agreed that the less the law interfered the better it would be for the health and growth of the community. Now we have recognised that it is essential for the protection of the great mass of the people that the law should be called in to guard them on almost every point of their lives. Legislation now affects the deepest interests of the people.

However, on that occasion his own remedy to 'the suffering in the large towns of England and amid the mountains of Wales, at Bethesda and Llanberis' was 'all-round delegation and devolution' – which he saw as a middle way between Tory oligarchy and 'Mr Keir Hardie's proposals for a social revolution' (*North Wales Observer*, 18 December 1896).

Nevertheless, the need for some legislation to deal with poverty and foul living conditions was a theme that he reiterated. On 1 November 1905, shortly before Balfour resigned as Prime Minister, Lloyd George said in Glasgow:

> When they had thirteen millions dwelling in that condition in the richest country in the world, it was strange that they should say that there was no change required. It would be one of the first duties that Liberalism must undertake – a change that would lift the people above that position . . .
>
> The old idea was the less legislation the better. . . . Unfortunately – probably he ought to say fortunately – the vast majority of the people of this country had come to the conclusion that, when they found a man hopeless and trodden under foot in the terrible struggle for existence, and when the man was too weak to struggle for himself, it was the business of the community to lend him a helping hand. (*Glasgow Herald*, 2 November 1905)

In this speech there is both the declaration of a need for state action and the limitation that it should not interfere with instances where the needy were capable of self-help.

In his Glasgow speech Lloyd George declared that he had a 'list of

Bills which all sections of the Liberal Party were agreed should be legislated upon' and that to do so 'would take ten years, i.e. two Parliaments'. But he declined to give his list, saying that if he did 'one man would ask how he left out this, and another why he included that' (*Glasgow Herald*, 2 November 1905). In fact, his notes survive and the list comprises 15 items, of which he deemed seven to be 'purely provincial': 'Education (England), Scotland, Ireland. Temperance. Land Question (towns), (country). Irish Land. Welsh Disestablishment. Scotch Disestablishment. Irish Local Government. Old Age Pensions. Miners' Eight Hours. Local Taxation. Extension of Local Government' (Lloyd George Papers, A/5/1). It is notable that the 1906—11 measures on behalf of children, the sick and those unemployed do not feature in his ten-year programme.

As for the provision of old-age pensions, it was a measure that he had long supported, albeit intermittently. His former hero Joseph Chamberlain brought forward a contributory pension plan in April 1891, and in the 1892 General Election Lloyd George spoke up for pensions but denounced Chamberlain's contributory scheme. Instead he called for a fund to be established to pay for them, urging 'let ground rents be taxed, let excessive pensions and salaries be reduced, and let the Royal Family be allowed just enough to keep up their dignity while they are with us.' He returned to the subject in the 1895 election, when the Unionists again made promises to introduce pensions. Then Lloyd George proposed to pay for them by increasing the newly introduced death duties, by using the tithe and by initiating various land taxes. He next took up the issue when be became a member of a House of Commons Select Committee on 'The Aged Deserving Poor', which the Salisbury Government set up in March 1899 (Wrigley, 1976, p. 33). To this Lloyd George proposed that a five shilling (25p) pension be offered to all over 65 who had an income of no more than ten shillings (50p) a week, providing they had not been convicted of a significant crime or been in receipt of poor relief for a given period — and even then they could redeem themselves if they could show that they had been thrifty for a substantial period thereafter (Gilbert, 1987, pp. 176—7). Subsequently Lloyd George used the Government's failure to introduce old-age pensions as a stick with which to beat them.

So it is fair to observe that there was much in Lloyd George's political pronouncements before the 1906 election that suggests he was not so irredeemably attached to the old Liberal dogmas that he would be unlikely to support the Government if it acted in new ways to deal with poverty. Indeed, he had made ample comments to suggest that he was willing to support state action and to find the means to finance it.

Moreover, before 1906 Lloyd George was well aware of many of the developments in society and in politics which historians have seen as the pressures behind the reforms (Hay, 1975, esp. pp. 25–38). He recognized the inadequacies and harshnesses of the Poor Law, even with the modifications made to it in the decades after its amendment in 1834. He was well aware of the growth of the labour movement in Britain, and how on the Continent it had supplanted Liberal parties. In his speeches he drew on the findings of the social surveys by Booth and Rowntree which had astonished many middle-class people by their revelations of the scale of poverty that existed in Britain's cities. He himself was very much in tune with the arguments and language of those pressing for increased national efficiency, especially given the shocks to Britain of the Boer War.

But for the new Liberal Government, which took office in December 1905 on Balfour's resignation, the first priority was to reverse those measures which had outraged Liberal supporters. Free Trade merely had to be maintained, but legislation was needed for education and the drink trade. These imperatives were underlined by the massive parliamentary majority in the 1906 General Election, when the Liberals polled 49 per cent of the votes and their Labour allies a further 5.9 per cent to the Conservatives 43.6 per cent, receiving 400, 30 and 157 seats respectively. During the election nonconformists especially had been active in support of Liberal candidates, and Liberal candidates readily promised to support nonconformist causes. Asquith, for example, pledged that 'corrective' education legislation would be the Government's first priority (Russell, 1973, pp. 183–5; Machin, 1987, pp. 275–8). After the election there were at least 177 nonconformists among the Liberal and Labour MPs to help keep ministers up to the mark on their pledges (Koss, 1975, p. 228). Between 1906 and 1908 the Government did make three attempts to modify education in at least some of the ways desired by most nonconformists, and one attempt to alter the licensing legislation. But in these efforts they were thwarted by the huge Tory majority in the House of Lords.

As for Lloyd George, he naturally devoted much of his energy to his first ministerial post, President of the Board of Trade (1905–8). There he greatly enhanced his reputation. The *Sheffield Independent* in late August 1907 gave a characteristic judgement of the time: 'Mr Lloyd George continues to present the curious dual phenomenon of the fiery Hotspur on the platform and a shrewd go-ahead admin-istrator in the office and the legislative chamber.' On the platform he vigorously denounced the House of Lords for savaging the Education and other Bills, thereby repeatedly enraging the King. Campbell-Bannerman fairly commented in response to the King's complaints, 'In all business connected with this department and in the House of Commons work he is most conciliatory, but the combative spirit seems to get the better of him when he is talking about other subjects' (Rowland, 1975, pp. 187−90)

Indeed, at the Board of Trade Lloyd George pleased industrialists and trade unionists alike. Throughout his career his violent denunci-ations were mostly confined to landowners, not businessmen. At the Board of Trade he could develop his national efficiency inclinations. His attitude at the Board was well-expressed in his comments to some shipowners in November 1906, 'Personally I do not believe in introducing party politics into business. ... My predecessors have kept party politics out of the administration of trade and business of the nation. That is the only way to succeed.' Lloyd George's attitude to these areas of public life was comparable to Rosebery's belief in the desirability of non-partisan British foreign policy. During his time at the Board of Trade he introduced a series of measures − Census of Production Act, Merchant Shipping Act, Patents and Designs Act, Companies Act and Port of London Act − which were designed to help British industry and in some cases to remove unfair foreign competition. As Sir John Clapham has commented of several of these measures, while they did constitute 'economic nationalism' they were 'a sensible dose of it'.

Lloyd George also displayed his talents for industrial conciliation on three occasions, involving the railway, cotton and engineering industries. In the case of a threatened railway dispute in the autumn of 1907 he gained great kudos in bringing about a compromise settlement which, though it lasted only a few years, did avert an imminent strike. These activities as an industrial trouble-shooter brought him into contact for the first time with major trade unions and their leaders. His ability to deal with the labour movement was to be very important in his later career, especially as Minister of Munitions and as Prime Minister (Wrigley, 1976, pp. 47−60). His widely ap-plauded triumph in averting the major economic disruption of a national rail strike in 1907 and his success in piloting much legislation through Parliament were in marked contrast to the lack-lustre performances of several of his more senior colleagues. These achievements helped to ensure that he succeeded Asquith as Chancellor of the Exchequer when the latter formed a government on 8 April 1908 following the resignation through terminal illness of Campbell-Bannerman.

Lloyd George by this time was moving away from the old Radical issues. In January 1907 he warned his countrymen that an assault on the House of Lords would have to take precedence over Welsh disestablishment, adding injudiciously that 'the Welshmen who worried them into attending to anything else until the citadel has been stormed ought to be put in the guardroom.' Campbell-Bannerman's announcement that there would be no Welsh Disestablishment Bill in the 1908 Parliamentary Session set off a 'Welsh revolt' against the Government, and especially against Lloyd George, which took Lloyd George's most emotional oratory to assuage. Significantly, when warned in the autumn of 1908 that Ellis Griffith MP would try again to 'raise a storm in Wales' over the issue, Lloyd George observed: 'He imagines that the old question we had in 1894 – Disestablishment – would do now as then, not remembering that fifteen years have now gone by and a new nation and new questions have come to the surface. ... All is now social questions' (Morgan, 1963b, pp. 235–8; Gilbert, 1987, pp. 305–13).

Lloyd George's career reached its pre-war height in 1908–11 with his advocacy of social reform and radically changed means of paying for it within the limits of Free Trade finance. In the case of old-age pensions, he took over the issue from Asquith who had introduced it in his 1908 Budget as a money measure (and so not open to interference by the House of Lords). From the outset the Government intended the measure to be a first instalment – limited to persons over 70 of limited income. But financially it was a leap in the dark, with estimates of the cost of this non-contributory scheme ranging upwards from £6 million. Lloyd George had long been aware of the difficulties of financing pensions. Earlier, when commenting that the issue was very much alive, he had felt: 'I think it may not be impossible to find the funds, but that no doubt will involve *a review of that fiscal system which I have indicated as necessary and desirable at an earlier date* (notes for speeches, 23 May?; Lloyd George Papers, A/5/6). The problem of funding a scheme which would cost so much was fundamental both to the very limited nature of the scheme on offer and to political difficulties that arose from it.

Could Free Trade finance do it? Balfour, when suggesting that the cost was more likely to be £11.5 million, taunted Lloyd George in the House of Commons with the question, 'how within the limits of Free

Trade finance are you to get £11½ million?' (192, *H. C. Deb. 4s*, 185; 9 July 1908). Lloyd George was determined that it would be found, one way or another. On 12 May he had written to his brother, 'I am not going to increase taxation to pay old age pensions until I have exhausted all means of reducing expenditure' (George, 1958, p. 221). So he approached his Cabinet colleagues in search of cuts, pointing out in a memorandum of 19 May that 'we have repeatedly pledged ourselves, both before we took office and since, to a substantial reduction in expenditure. ...' He looked long and hard at the Government's army and navy expenditure, but decided that cuts of the necessary magnitude could not be made there, given the tensions with Germany. Nevertheless he happily told a Peace Congress meeting on 28 July that in the House of Lords there were 'noblemen who think we ought to save a little on pensions for old people in order to provide more money for armaments'. In contrast, he declared, 'My principle as Chancellor of the Exchequer is "less money for the production of suffering and more money for the reduction of suffering"' (*Daily News*, 29 July 1908). While hoping to encourage a 'naval holiday' when visiting Germany in August 1908, Lloyd George on his return had to recognize that substantial additional revenue would be needed. Indeed, contrary to his Cabinet Paper of 19 May, he told the Common six days later, 'we could not possibly have given pledges for a reduced expenditure when we contemplated social reform which involved increased expenditure' (189, *H. C. Deb. 4s*, 869).

The exigencies of this financial situation propelled him forward towards what was to become the 'People's Budget'. But there were other elements in his motivation. For Lloyd George politics was very much the art of the possible. Part of this involved right timing: knowing when to press a favoured policy and when to let it be. The need for substantial additional revenue for pensions and for battleships gave Lloyd George the opportunity to take up measures he had long favoured and ones which had been much aired by the more advanced wing of the Liberal Party.

Moreover, in taking over the issue of pensions from Asquith he appears to have come to reassess his own priorities in social welfare. He was not unduly impressed with pensions as a provision receiving a very high proportion of Government social funding. A few days after becoming Chancellor, Lloyd George told his friend D. R. Daniel that he did not feel old age to be 'the hardest burden. ... The tragedy that appeals most to me is seeing the workman whose strength is ebbing gradually, and yet because of his family burdens has to go every day to the quarry or factory' (Gilbert, 1987, pp. 338–9). He repeated his concern in his first major speech on the Old Age Pensions Bill in the Commons on 15 June 1908, stating that the problems of the sick, the infirm and the unemployed were 'problems with which it is the business of the state to deal' and were ones 'which the state has neglected too long' (190, *H. C. Deb. 4s*, 485). His concern about these issues was reinforced by his visit to Germany in the late summer of 1908.

Lloyd George's always well-tuned political antennae told him that the time was ripe for such measures. The Liberal Government could not afford to stay in the political doldrums as it had done in 1906 and 1907. In by-elections at Jarrow and Colne Valley in 1907 the electorate had looked to the Left. The cause of Tariff Reform remained a very potent threat on the Right. Younger men, such as Churchill and Masterman, were pressing the need for a bigger initiative in the area of social reform. Lloyd George was not a man to be left behind in pressing popular causes. Writing to his brother of the 1908 Budget (which included the pension provisions), Lloyd George observed, 'It is time we did something that appealed straight to the people – it will, I think, help to stop this electoral rot, and that is most necessary' (George, 1958, p. 220). From 1909 to 1911 his campaigns for his first Budget and then for further social welfare measures did reinvigorate both the Government and the Liberal Party in the country.

Lloyd George's 1909 Budget was innovative, as Bruce Murray has observed, because it 'was founded on the new principle that taxation should serve as a major instrument of long-term social policy'. Moreover, as he has rightly argued, the Budget indicated the Government's 'preparedness to ensure that direct taxes should be responsible for a measurably larger share of taxation than regressive indirect taxes. It ensured this by methods designed to increase very considerably the rate of taxation for the wealthy and simultaneously protect the white-collar, small-business and professional middle classes' (Murray, 1980, pp. 15–16). In this Lloyd George's fiscal measures were in very marked contrast to tariffs, which in Germany had been the means by which the government had avoided directly taxing the privileged and which through the unfairness of the resulting heavy indirect taxes (including higher food prices) had contributed to the rise of the Socialist Party (SPD). Lloyd George's Budget was very much an attack on the British *Junkers* (landowners). Even in such famous verbal assaults on privilege, as at Limehouse in East London on 30 July 1909, his remarks were aimed at the landed interest and not at the middle class.

44

In the 1909 Budget Lloyd George sought to raise an additional £16 million. In his preparations he allowed £8,750,000 for old-age pensions and an additional £2,823,000 for naval expenditure (within a total of over £35 million for the navy). He proposed to raise £10,200,000 by direct taxation, £3,400,000 from indirect taxation and to take the remainder from the Sinking Fund. He gained his extra income by raising income tax from 1s to 1s 2d (from 5 to 6p) in the £ on unearned incomes and on earned incomes over £3,000 a year; by introducing super-tax at 6d (2.5p) in the £ on incomes over £5,000; by increasing death-duties to a maximum of 15 (instead of 8) per cent on estates worth over £1 million; by bringing in taxes on motor vehicles and petrol; by substantially raising the tax on liquor licenses, and adding to the duties on spirits and tobacco; and by introducing a number of land taxes. The land taxes were the most controversial aspect, but this was more to do with them being seen as 'the thin end of the wedge' — this particular wedge being land valuation (and thereby providing the potential means for future drastic measures) — than because of the modest sums actually levied under this budget. On the expenditure side he provided children's allowances of £10 per child under 16 for all incomes under £500 (Murray, 1980, pp. 127–8, 152–63).

In the cases of the taxes on land and licences, Lloyd George was putting measures in his Finance Bill that were ardently desired by many Liberals yet had received brusque treatment in the past from the House of Lords. Asquith's final Budget had shown the way with old-age pensions. In the fourth year of the Parliament, the licensing proposals would delight nonconformists dismayed by the loss of the 1908 Licensing Bill, just as the land proposals would please such Radical bodies as the United Committee for the Taxation of Land Values, not to mention some 400 Liberal MPs who had petitioned Campbell-Bannerman to introduce such taxation and who had been angered by the Lords' savaging of the Land Values (Scotland) Bill of 1907 (Emy, 1973, pp. 209–10; Douglas, 1976, pp. 142–3).

Though at one time many historians felt that Lloyd George set out to provoke the House of Lords (for example, Dangerfield, 1935, pp. 19–20), the generally accepted view now is that he was out to circumvent it. After George Riddell, the owner of the *News of the World*, had breakfasted with Lloyd George on 24 November 1908 he noted that the Chancellor 'ridiculed the rumour that the Peers would or could interfere with or reject the Budget' (Riddell, 1934, p. 10). Later, when rejection seemed to be likely, Lloyd George appears to have taken the view that the Liberals would gain either way. If the

45

Peers did reject it, they would provide an excellent election issue, whereas if they did not, the Peers would be humiliated and the Liberal Government would have had révenge for the Lords' actions of 1892–5 and 1906–8. In this spirit, from late July 1909 Lloyd George goaded the Peers and made much of the fact that rejection would reveal that they were 'forcing a revolution', rather than that his Budget was revolutionary, as Rosebery and others complained.

All in all, the 'People's Budget' and the move towards social issues reveal Lloyd George exhibiting the same approach to politics as he had shown in 1885 and often in the 1890s. That is, he firmly believed that Liberalism under duress needed attractive programmes and controversy to galvanize the electorate and so ensure that potential supporters turned out and voted Liberal.

He himself campaigned around the country with great vigour, as did Churchill. J. L. Garvin, the editor of *The Observer*, dubbed their efforts 'a double Midlothian'. Lloyd George appears to have made two alternative predictions of the outcome of the election: either a combined anti-Unionist majority of about 173 or of about 126 (Blewett, 1972, pp. 107, 131; Riddell, 1934, p. 18). In the event, the lower estimate proved to be nearer to the actual anti-Unionist majority of 124 (which was still 42 should the Irish Nationalist MPs abstain). However, the Liberal Government was again dependent in the Commons on the goodwill of the Irish Nationalist MPs, just as the previous Liberal Governments of 1886 and 1892–5 had been. Lloyd George felt that the new majority was sufficient mandate to proceed with the Budget and to deal with the House of Lords. However, some of his Cabinet colleagues were more defeatist.

Soon after the January 1910 election Lloyd George and his colleagues were disconcerted to learn that Asquith had failed to secure the King's agreement to create sufficient new peers to overcome the House of Lords' veto, should that become necessary. This discovery was especially embarrassing for Lloyd George who had said at the National Liberal Club on 3 December 1909, at the outset of his General Election campaign, 'For my part, I would not remain a member of a Liberal Cabinet for one hour unless I knew that the Cabinet had determined not to hold office after the next general election unless full powers are accorded to it . . . [to remove the veto].' (This was a passage which he carefully omitted from the published collection of his speeches which went to the printers in August 1910; Lloyd George, 1910, pp. 176–91.) Lacking such powers from the King and faced with the Irish Nationalist MPs' attitude of 'no veto, no Budget', Asquith and many of his colleagues seriously contemplated resignation.

Lloyd George remained full of fight. He told Herbert Lewis on 25 February 1910:

> that but for him and Winston Churchill the Cabinet would have resigned this afternoon. He said that they were thinking too much of their own feelings, forgetting that they were the trustees of a great cause.   (Diary entry; J. H. Lewis Papers, 10/231/91)

Lloyd George first of all tried to do a deal. He attempted to gain Irish Nationalist support for his Budget by offering in return concessions to the Irish within it (notably over whisky duties). But he soon realized that such concessions were 'trivial' compared to the main issue of the veto (Gilbert, 1987, pp. 406–8). Instead, he successfully pushed the Cabinet on 13 April to agree to demand from the King that a further election would be accompanied by guarantees that 'in the new Parliament . . . the judgement of the people expressed at the elections would be carried into law.' The whole episode of guarantees revealed indecision and lack of political judgement on Asquith's part, and a determination on Lloyd George's part to reach his goal one way or another.

Indeed, to Lloyd George the political near-deadlock of 1910 opened up all manner of possibilities, or at least it stimulated him into airing various speculations. To Herbert Lewis, when testifying that he was still 'a single chamber man', he suggested that that solution to the clash between the Houses of Commons and Lords would only be politically feasible 'if the plan were daring enough to attract the Labour and Irish men' (Lewis diary, 19 February 1910; J. H. Lewis Papers, 10/231/89). In contrast, two months later, shortly before Asquith and the Cabinet agreed to demand the guarantees from the King, he speculated to Charles Masterman that if Asquith resigned and he formed a government he would bring in 'businessmen, Sir Christopher Furness, Alfred Mond, and such, which would carry enormous weight in the country' (Masterman, 1939, p. 160). The recovery by the Cabinet of its collective nerve on 13 April ended these speculations. But with King Edward VII's death on 6 May a new situation arose.

The King's death provided the occasion for a conference of Liberal and Unionist leaders to attempt to resolve the constitutional crisis. Lloyd George appears to have tried to claim the credit for this initiative when speaking to his closest associates. Lucy Masterman noted later, 'It cannot be too much emphasised that the Conference was entirely his idea' (Masterman, 1939, p. 163). But more probably it stemmed on the Liberal side from conversations between the Master of Elibank, the Chief Whip, and George V when the latter was still Prince of Wales – but which Lloyd George would have known about either directly from Elibank or through the involvement of his two associates, Rufus Isaacs and Churchill (Murray, 1945, pp. 46–7; Gollin, 1960, pp. 182–7).

Whatever his role in bringing about the Constitutional Conference, Lloyd George was a key figure in its deliberations between June and mid-November 1910. He refused to be sidetracked by Lord Lansdowne's suggestion of House of Lords reform. Just as Michael Foot and Enoch Powell were to unite against such reform in 1969, so Lloyd George acted with the Earl of Cawdor in 1910 (Lewis diary, 17 July 1910; J. H. Lewis Papers 10/231/96). Lloyd George also refused to allow concessions to be made to the Unionists which would undermine the Liberals' commitment to Home Rule, making it clear that if too much were offered he would resign from the Government (Fair, 1980, pp. 86–102).

However, he tried to go much further than the remit of the Constitutional Conference, hoping to set the constitutional deadlock in a wider perspective and to solve it as part of a wide-ranging package of compromise measures on most major political issues. In sounding out his ideas on D. R. Daniel he gave the impression that 'there were potentialities of a Grand Coalition Government on the doorstep, with the great aim before it of tackling the great social questions that were not ripe for settlement.' To such a Welsh supporter he naturally indicated 'poverty, intemperance, land' as being among his priorities (B. B. Gilbert, 1987, p. 414). He formulated his proposals in a secret memorandum drawn up on 17 August 1910 (with a supplementary memorandum on 29 October). In this memorandum he suggested that a broad coalition government would be able to deal in a non-party spirit with such issues as housing, drink, education, the land, health insurance, unemployment, the restructuring of the Poor Law, local government, trade, inland transport, conscription, Imperial defence and Ireland (Searle, 1971, pp. 177–98; Scally, 1975, pp. 375–86).

In trying to bring both sides together to negotiate on such issues Lloyd George used all his guile; it was a case of his 'writing in a Liberal sense to his colleagues and talking in a Conservative sense to

48

his opponents' (Searle, 1971, p. 189). Nevertheless, in so doing he was making a genuine attempt to break out of various political impasses. He wanted not only to resolve the constitutional problem but also to clear aside the old nonconformist issues and Home Rule, to overcome the obstacle of industrial insurance companies to his insurance plans and to get to grips with land issues. In the case of Ireland, he was clearly hoping to remove the resolution of the issue from the control of the Irish Nationalist MPs and to revert back to his old favourite panacea of Home Rule All Round (Scally, 1975, p. 189). It is also quite likely that, similarly, he hoped to resist Labour Party pressure to reverse the Osborne Judgement, which had effectively banned the use of trade union funds for political purposes (Wrigley, 1985, pp. 138–44).

Lloyd George gave some public indication of his thinking in a speech at the City Temple on 17 October 1910. In it he paid tribute to Joseph Chamberlain and the issue of Tariff Reform for helping 'to call attention to a number of real crying evils festering among us' and went on to declare that for such problems 'the remedy must be a bold one. ... The time has come for a thorough overhauling of our national and imperial conditions.' Even in this guarded form his comments caused a stir in Radical circles. The *Yorkshire Herald* on 18 October commented, 'Many Liberals will rub their eyes when they read Mr Lloyd George's statement. Such a statement is calculated ... to send an ardent party man like the ex-Liberal member for York [Hamar Greenwood] into fits.' The Unionists were not slow to realize that in promoting such a scheme Lloyd George was putting his Radical reputation at risk.

However, Balfour refused to make any substantial compromise on Ireland, thereby ensuring that both Lloyd George's secret coalition proposals and the Constitutional Conference came to nothing (Shannon, 1988, pp. 153–8). As a result, a second General Election took place in 1910, in which Lloyd George attacked his opponents with his customary vigour. The outcome of the December election was that the anti-Unionist majority rose from 122 to 126 (with the Liberals remaining dependent on the Irish and Labour) and subsequently, in 1911, the Parliament Bill was passed.

Lloyd George's conciliatory approach to his opponents in the midst of party strife was not a one-off aberration. He made a similar move during the heated rows over Balfour's Education Bill of 1902. He was to do the same during the tensions over Ireland in 1913–14. At the Oxford Union on 21 November 1913 he declared:

49

Party has become an essential part of government. Many have tried to get their ideas through without associating themselves with Party the they have always failed, because party government is an essential part of the government of this country. You might as well try to cross from here to Vancouver without using the machinery of transport . . . as to try to get anything through in this country without party government. I sometimes honestly deplore it. There are many things which, if you could get a party truce for five years, you could get through and transform this land. (*Oxford Chronicle*, 28 November 1913)

At this time he was following up suggestions from F. E. Smith who, on 26 September 1913, had dangled the bait before him that 'if a conference was held on H. R. [Home Rule] it might and ought to be extended to cover H. of L. [House of Lords] reform and the Land. From such a conference anything could follow.' Lloyd George joined Churchill in making soundings as to the possibility of an Irish settlement involving the exclusion of Ulster from Home Rule. In Lloyd George's case, as was usual in his negotiating technique, he stretched the truth to the limit and beyond in trying to persuade the Irish Nationalists to compromise (Jalland, 1980, pp. 145–75; Campbell, 1983, pp. 340–2). In the end, as in 1910, no compromise was achieved on Ireland. But in responding to Smith, Lloyd George both publicly and privately made clear his wish for compromise to achieve his aims. To Smith on 6 October 1913 he had written, 'You know how anxious I have been for years to work with you and few others on your side. I have always realised that our differences have been very artificial and do not reach the realities' (Lloyd George Papers, C/3/7/2).

When Lloyd George came to press ahead with what became the National Insurance Act 1911, he again tried to appeal to a cross-party spirit, just as he had done in the summer of 1910. He did so publicly when he introduced the Bill in the House of Commons on 4 May 1911, and he followed up these remarks privately by using Garvin as an intermediary with Balfour. But without success. Later, when it became a matter of major political controversy, Lloyd George made much of his efforts to be non-partisan. On 14 October, at Whitefields Tabernacle, Lloyd George declared, 'I have endeavoured in all sincerity to make this a non-party measure.' He went on to say that he had offered several times to listen to constructive suggestions for improvements from the Conservatives:

If my offer had been accepted ... we should have had a Bill commanding the votes of all parties, reflecting a credit not on one party or on one Minister, but on the common sense, constructive capacity and governing power of our race and of our men. ... It would have formed such a valuable precedent. No offer of the kind had ever been made before by a Minister. We asked them to assist us to see how we could save the wretched in the land. They would have nothing to do with it. (Lloyd George, 1912, pp. 221–2)

In this Lloyd George was probably in part covering his back politically, given the possibility that his secret coalition proposals could become public knowledge at any time. But he was above all genuinely keen to square as many political forces as he could in order to ensure further legislative action against an aspect of poverty which he himself had highlighted during the debates over old-age pensions.

Lloyd George had a decisive role in the form that the legislation took. W. J. Braithwaite, the very earnest Treasury official who played a major part in preparing the way for National Insurance for Lloyd George, paid tribute to him after the measure reached the statute book:

Looking back on these two and a half months I am more and more impressed with the Chancellor's curious genius, his capacity to listen, judge if a thing is practicable, deal with the immediate point, deferring all unnecessary decision and keeping every road open till he sees which is really best. Working for any other man I must inevitably have acquiesced in some scheme which would not have been as good as this one, and I am very glad now that he tore up so many proposals of my own and other people which were put forward as solutions ... (Bunbury, 1957, p. 143)

For fiscal reasons Lloyd George became attached to the notion of insurance as a way of dealing with aspects of poverty due to sickness and unemployment primarily. It was a means to his end which avoided both the Chamberlain route of tariffs and another round of innovative tax proposals such as had followed the non-contributory old-age pensions; and it would also be seen to reinforce the virtue of thrift.

While Churchill clearly took the lead in heralding the need for a new and bold approach to the problem of unemployment, notably in a letter entitled 'The Untrodden Field of Politics' published in the

*Nation* on 7 March 1908, there has been some discussion as to whether Churchill influenced Lloyd George over insurance or vice versa. The weight of evidence points to Lloyd George taking the lead by looking at insurance in Germany. As Professor Hennock has shown, he appears to have become interested in learning from Germany after the Liberal MP Harold Cox had highlighted the nature of German and Austrian insurance schemes during the course of the old-age pension debates in May 1907 (Hennock, 1987, pp. 143–7, 163–4). Lloyd George visited Germany in August 1908 and there discussed the insurance system with Bethmann Hollweg, then Minister of the Interior. Speaking on his return, he highlighted the health insurance aspect of the German scheme rather than its approach to the provision of old-age pensions (B. B. Gilbert, 1966, pp. 291–3). Thereafter, while he drew on the example of the German insurance scheme, he made much play of outdoing it. This he achieved by making employers' contributions 3*d* (1.2p) a week, instead of an original plan of 2*d* (0.8p) a week, the additional money funding maternity benefits and improved financial resources for medical treatment. The final version of unemployment insurance owed as much to British precedents as to German and other foreign examples. Professor Hennock has commented, 'Just as unemployment insurance was undoubtedly constructed on the basis of trade union experience and practice, so health insurance took shape in relation to the experience and practice of Friendly Societies' (Hennock, 1987, pp. 177–8, 189–90).

As well as being willing to draw on their experience, Lloyd George was also concerned to appease the powerful vested interests which felt threatened by the prospect of national insurance. The friendly societies and industrial insurance societies were, not surprisingly, very concerned at the prospect of state competition in their areas, especially in health insurance. On this, representatives of the friendly societies expressed the fear to Lloyd George at an early stage that 'the establishment of such a system in England must "kill" voluntary organisations like ours.' Similarly the trade unions which provided unemployment benefits were suspicious of state activity in this area. Moreover, many of the more Radical trade unionists disliked provision of unemployment and health benefits being funded by flat-rate schemes paid by working people, wishing instead for a scheme funded (like pensions) from general taxation. In the case of the British Medical Association, many of its influential wealthy doctors feared that Lloyd George's health proposals would adversely affect their private practices.

52

Lloyd George exercised his considerable political skills to assuage much of the pressure-group opposition to state insurance. He bought the support of the friendly societies by making them the agents of the state scheme, thereby extending their business much wider among the working class. Similar concessions to the trade unions undermined most opposition on their part to unemployment and health insurance and, indeed, led to spectacular increases in membership of a few unions in sectors with hitherto low membership (Gilbert, 1966, pp. 279−80, 285−6). In the case of the industrial insurance companies, they and their collectors effectively campaigned to secure from candidates in the 1910 General Election pledges to safeguard their interests. As a result Lloyd George abandoned his plans to provide pensions for widows and orphans and had to allow the insurance companies to join the friendly societies as health insurance administrators. Finally, after the Bill was passed, Lloyd George needed to gain the support of the majority of the medical profession for the measure. This he achieved by a number of concessions, but notably by ensuring that the fees provided by insurance committees were higher than the average hitherto received by doctors, thereby splitting the majority of the medical profession from the belligerent, highly paid specialists (Gilbert, 1966, pp. 318−416).

In manoeuvring round such powerful pressure groups, and also in squaring the Labour and Irish Nationalist MPs, Lloyd George displayed his formidable political skills. At the end of the day he achieved a major measure of social insurance. The first part of the Act (unemployment) was experimental, covering two and a quarter million workers in several trades which were predictably prone to cyclical unemployment, and providing 7$s$ (35p) benefit per week for a maximum of 15 weeks per year. In the case of the second part (health), the coverage was of all regularly employed adults with incomes below £160 per annum. They would be eligible to receive sickness benefit of 10$s$ (50p) (men) or 7$s$ 6$d$ (37.5p) (women) for up to 26 weeks in a year (and thereafter receive disability benefit of 5$s$ (25p) a week) and to receive medical treatment, and for wives to receive maternity benefit. Both parts involved compulsory insurance: in the case of unemployment the worker paid $2\frac{1}{2}d$ (1p), the employer $2\frac{1}{2}d$ and the state 2$d$ (0.8p); in the case of health insurance the amounts were 4$d$ (1.6p) for men and 3$d$ for women, with 3$d$ (1.2p) and 2$d$ (0.8p) from the employer and the state respectively − Lloyd George's famous 'ninepence for fourpence'.

In these measures old Liberal attitudes blended with newer, less moralistic ones. William Braithwaite, the civil servant most involved

53

in drafting the national health insurance measure, made the revealing comment in his memoirs: 'My own experience in boys' club work was convincing to me that working people ought to pay something! It gave them a feeling of self-respect, and what cost nothing was not valued' (Bunbury, 1957, p. 80). Yet Lloyd George, attracted by the insurance principle (which made benefits a right to those who had paid the premiums), was also firm that the measure should not be used to police people's personal conduct. He rejected the notion that payments should be withheld from those who were sick through their own negligence, and had added to the Bill a clause laying down 'that medical treatment shall be given without regard to cause or nature of disease' (Fraser, 1973, p. 150). However, not surprisingly, those on low wages proved to be more mindful of the increased pressure on their family budgets arising from the contribution than of the benefits, and the measure proved to be widely unpopular.

One feature of the final version of Lloyd George's health insurance provision was the accumulation of an insurance reserve fund. In a Cabinet memorandum it was stated, 'It is proposed to use part of the funds for making loans under the Housing Acts.' As Bentley Gilbert has commented in his masterful study of national insurance, these words pointed the way to 'a third great welfare project . . . [just] as health insurance had been a logical extension of pensions' (Gilbert, 1966, p. 347). Housing reform was an adjunct of land reform, one of the most consistent aspects of Lloyd George's political career and one which was still a potent issue in Radical circles. It was also an aspect of rural regeneration, which he hoped to foster in his People's Budget of 1909 through the setting up of a Development Fund.

By making the land issue, in all its ramifications, the most prominent one in British politics, and not Home Rule or Tariff Reform, Lloyd George hoped to revive both the Government's fortunes and the fervour of its supporters. He had tried this with some degree of success in the 1909 Budget. In June 1912, assured of funding by wealthy Liberal supporters, Lloyd George set up his unofficial Land Enquiry Committee. It had Asquith's backing, for he shared Lloyd George's concern about the weakening of Liberal support in rural areas. When Lloyd George launched his campaign on 11 October 1913, he focused his attention not only on housing and rural development but above all on low rural wages. He had been much interested in extending the principle of minimum wages to other workers after the 1912 mining dispute had been settled in March by legislation establishing this principle for the coal industry (Grigg, 1985, pp. 21 –

3, 36–8). As always when dealing with rural issues, Lloyd George was careful to menace landlords but not farmers, to whom he offered the prospect of rent appeals and security of tenure as well as reassurance that the improved wages would be taken from rents (Emy, 1971, pp. 43, 49–60; Offer, 1981, pp. 375–7). Quite clearly, Lloyd George's campaign in the traditional Tory heartlands greatly worried much of the Conservative leadership and MPs. The members of a Conservative working party on the land warned Bonar Law that 'the agricultural voter might be inclined to think that he had to choose between sacrificing Ulster and sacrificing his own private interest' (Offer, 1981, pp. 378–83). It also revived moribund Liberal Associations and appears to have reduced the size of the swing against the Government on the eve of the First World War (Packer, 1991, pp. 150–1).

Lloyd George was less effective in campaigning on the land issue as it affected urban communities. This was largely due to the facts that the separate committee set up to provide an urban report only did so in April 1914 and that the carrying out of site valuations was slowly and poorly done. But it was also due in part to Lloyd George's lesser regard for urban life and his taste for the old panacea of 'Back to the Land'. He had expounded this view frequently before taking office. Thus in Scotland on 19 November 1903 he was reported as saying:

It was a serious thing for a country when the people were driven from the healthiest of all employment, from the employment which, above all, gave muscle to frame – driven ... into the town, crowded into the town, there eventually to produce slums, misery and squalor. Such a state of affairs was a serious thing for a country, and it ought to be one of the duties of any statesman to consider the problem and to decide some means of restoring the people to the land and to the healthy occupation that they formerly occupied. (*Falkirk Herald*, 21 November 1903)

Pressure had grown for changes in local government finance. Lloyd George saw this as an important area for reform, and he appears to have made promises to Liberal back-benchers committed to the single tax (that is, land) in June 1913 to abolish the current system of rating and substitute 'a rate levied on the land value alone'. While Lloyd George back-pedalled on making this change suddenly, it does seem – as Avner Offer has commented – that Lloyd George originally planned 'a gradual build-up of publicity in the summer of 1914, in

55

anticipation of a dramatic reforming budget in 1915, followed perhaps by a general election' (Offer, 1981, p. 393 and also pp. 384–400).

In the event, Lloyd George tried to rush ahead and introduce new taxes in his 1914 Budget, rashly trying to introduce provisional rating relief ahead of the proper valuation, when he was prompted by the needs of increased naval expenditure to raise substantially greater revenue. The result was a disaster for this aspect of his Budget. It was withdrawn after the Speaker ruled out of order his initial inclusion of his local government finance measures within his Budget and after a revolt of some 40 right-wing Liberal MPs (M. Gilbert, 1968; Murray, 1990). Nevertheless, Lloyd George's 1914 Budget did mark, like the 1909 Budget, a major shift towards direct taxes. And although his plans for local government finance reform came to grief in 1914, he did succeed (in the Housing Act 1914) in allocating £4 million for housing loans to local authorities and other agencies.

Before the outbreak of war in 1914 Lloyd George was still full of fight and of determination to push forward with reforms. As in the 1880s and the 1890s he saw that the best hope of reviving Liberal fortunes was to take on his opponents by challenging them with a programme that would hearten the Liberal Party activists. By the last decade before the war he had realized that the way to generate such enthusiasm now lay in innovatory social reforms, not in the old Radical issues of the late nineteenth century. Moreover, as he liked to say, his sympathies were with 'the underdog', with working people who had no effective organizations to act on their behalf.

# 4

# From 'Pro-Boer' to 'The Man Who Won the War'

In late 1918 Lloyd George was widely deemed to be one of the main architects of British victory in the Great War. In the popular press he was dubbed 'The Man Who Won the War'. Such a view was also shared by many discerning 'insiders' of British politics. Balfour, for one, was later quick to testify to the vital importance of Lloyd George's contribution to the achievement of Germany's defeat. Yet 15 to 18 years earlier he had been condemned in similar circles for lacking patriotism and for being a 'Pro-Boer', someone near to being a traitor. In recent years historians have carefully rebutted any lingering doubts as to whether Lloyd George was ever a 'Little Englander', and so anti-Empire, or even a pacifist (for example, Grigg, 1973, 1974; Fry, 1977).

The Boer War was the issue which made Lloyd George into a national figure. During it he became identified as one of the leading opponents of the war. And, to his family and acquaintances, he often revealed considerable sympathy for the Boers in their struggle against the might of the British army. In going against the dominant war mood Lloyd George had to exercise all his skills, including verbal ability, to fight for his political survival. In the face of often massive political hostility he displayed all the characteristic ambiguities or dualities which often resided in his character: such as pugnacious attacks on opponents, yet a willingness to be conciliatory; claims to be a greater imperialist than the government, yet appeals to the non-conformist conscience against war; praise of Rosebery and even Salisbury, yet invocations of Cobden and Bright.

But before the Boer War commenced in October 1899, many of

Lloyd George's later patriotic and Empire-minded sentiments were in evidence, albeit often mixed with traditional old Radical notions. He had said a great deal on the subject of patriotism in the early 1890s when he had been exalting Welsh nationalism. He frequently deemed patriotism to be 'a powerful element planted in the human breast for the elevation of mankind' (*Birkenhead News*, 6 February 1892). He eulogized nationalism. Thus in early 1892 at Pontypridd he observed:

> Welshmen on the hills of Wales would die for a national feeling; Irishmen had gone to the scaffold for love of country; even the wild Nubian man of the desert fought, fell and left his bones to bleach on the sands of the great Sahara for national sentiment. There was nothing which governed the whole world from Pole to Pole like the love of country. A government which did not utilise this tremendous force in nature was but a travesty of government after all. Patriotism was not bigotry or narrowness. (*Pontypridd Chronicle*, 15 January 1892)

Even then he linked Welsh nationalism with a wider Empire patriotism. Thus at a meeting in the Guild Hall at Carnarvon on 28 May 1891, he commented:

> As Welsh Liberals we are Imperialists because we are nationalists. ... We know ... that by the sum of the success, prosperity and happiness attained by little Wales, the great Empire of which she is a part will be the more glorious. (*Carnarvon Herald*, 29 May 1891)

Lloyd George would have been unusual among nationalists in Europe if his espousal of nationalism had not been accompanied by a degree of pugnacity. In his case he reserved it for the more powerful states, reacting with vigour to what he saw as provocative actions, but applied more Cobdenite sentiments to smaller nations. On 1 July 1893, at Taff's Well, he declared:

> No true Liberal need be afraid of nationality, for true patriotism never deserted the cause of liberty, but had always fought for it. It was only when patriotism interfered with the affairs of other nations that it began to tyrannise. (*Pontypridd Chronicle*, 7 July 1893)

It came naturally to him during the Boer War to appeal to his constituents as members of 'a little nation which had fought for centuries for their rights not to take part in the work of extinguishing these two little republics of South Africa' (*North Wales Observer*, 29 April 1900). This was a significant line of argument that he made at the time, not largely a later construct by him and his brother, as one overzealous recent attempt at revisionism has suggested (Gilbert, 1987, p. 179).

Before the Boer War Lloyd George occasionally used foreign-affairs issues as sticks with which to beat the Salisbury Government. He argued that in reality the Government was weak when dealing with major powers and was prone to give way. Instead, he argued that Britain should stand up for its rights, pursuing these by means of arbitration rather than war. Thus at the time of the Fashoda incident in 1898, when Britain and France clashed over the Upper Nile, Lloyd George asserted that in Britain there was a consensus determined not to surrender the Sudan after the expenditure of much blood and treasure, jeered at the Government for being willing to concede too much (observing at Haworth that it was lucky that the French had not asked for Yorkshire), yet making it clear that he did not wish to clash with 'the only power on the continent with a democratic constitution' (*Bradford Observer*, 2 November 1898; *Manchester Guardian*, 19 January 1899). Earlier, in 1896, he condemned Salisbury for attempting to coerce Venezuela, for refusing arbitration and then for giving way when faced with major pressure from the United States. Lloyd George's response was to be similar when the Russian fleet fired on British North Sea fishing vessels off the Dogger Bank in October 1904. This he denounced as 'a most insolent and unjustifiable action', but applauded Lord Lansdowne's decision to go to arbitration (Fry, 1977, pp. 33 and 35; *South Wales Daily News*, 30 November 1896; *North Wales Observer*, 28 October 1904).

As well as following the Gladstonian line on the desirability of arbitration in international disputes, Lloyd George also broadly condemned the ethos of Salisbury's foreign policy as being 'inspired by commercial principles', not morality and duty. In early 1898, at Colwyn Bay, he contrasted the decline from Gladstone's day of 'Britain the crusader . . . the Britain that had been the missionary' to 'Britain the peddler, Britain the huxterer' (*Weekly News*, 21 January 1896). He suggested a role for himself, observing, 'If there is one thing that the Liberals want, it is a man on the Front Bench to unmask the pretensions of the electro-plated Rome, its peddling imperialism and its tin Caesar.' Of the last, Chamberlain, he had also commented that he had met his match in the Transvaal with Kruger

(*South Wales Daily News*, 5 February 1898; *Cambria Daily Leader*, 15 December 1898).

Lloyd George's attitude to the outbreak of the war was consistent with his broad approach to Salisbury's foreign policy and in line with his suspicion of Chamberlain's activities in particular. He was in Canada when war appeared inevitable. From there he wrote to his brother a letter which was read out at a public protest meeting against the war held in Carnarvon on 6 October, at which John Morley was the main speaker. In the version of his letter which reached his constituents via the local press, Lloyd George was reported to have written, 'The prospect oppresses us with sorrow, and I shall protest with all the vehemence I can command against this blackguardish action which is perpetrated in the name of human freedom' (*North Wales Observer*, 13 October 1899; see also George, 1958, p. 177). Lloyd George was to argue that in South Africa Britain was playing the part of an aggressive Great Power and that the Government should have been able to resolve any outstanding differences with the small Boer states by peaceful means. Indeed, at Carmarthen in late November 1899 he said with reference to the pre-war negotiations, 'They were at war with every proposal accepted.' Then he was also reported as making a comment which summed up his attitude, 'He did not mean to say that under no conditions should they fight, but he could say that the case must be an overwhelming one indeed before they did it' (*The Welshman*, 1 December 1899).

In the early period of the Boer War Lloyd George concentrated his attacks on the lack of a real need for war and the waste of resources involved. He was careful not to criticize the bravery of the British troops and, indeed, went out of his way to praise the gallantry of the Welsh regiments. Later on he did attack the conduct of the war, criticizing Lord Roberts and Haig as well as Chamberlain (though notably showing restraint in his treatment of Milner, a hero of the Liberal Imperialists).

In his policy of 'go for Joe', Lloyd George was displaying his characteristic belief that the best means of defence is offence. He had shown this before in the way he had personalized his attacks when opposing the Agricultural Rating Bill in 1896, making much of the monetary gains accruing from the policy for the ministers concerned. In August 1900 he raised in the Commons, with considerable effect, a finding of a Parliamentary Select Committee on War Office Contracts that there had been special treatment for the armaments firm of Kynoch's, of which Chamberlain's brother was chairman. In this instance he was responding in kind to Chamberlain who had effectively smeared all opponents of the war just before the calling of a General Election, by stating that some letters from MPs to Boer leaders had been captured. He gave no names or details but only the opinion that they were 'not proper letters to have written' (Grigg, 1973, pp. 267–70). Moreover, there was a case to be answered, and not only regarding Kynoch's. For soon after Chamberlain had denied in the Commons that he had direct or indirect interest in supplying war material to the Government, it became public (through the investigations of the *Morning Leader*) that one son, Austen, then Civil Lord of the Admiralty, was a major shareholder, another son, Neville, was managing director, and his wife and two daughters were also shareholders in another firm, Hoskins & Sons, which had contracts with the War Office and the Admiralty (Searle, 1987, pp. 52–7). But Lloyd George was also returning to an issue he had tried to stir before: the link between Chamberlain and Kynoch's. In July 1895, during the General Election, he had raised its position as a government contractor and in July 1896 he had questioned whether it forbade its employees to join trade unions (*North Wales Observer*, 12 July 1896; 42 *H.C. Deb. 3s*, 1642, 16 July 1896).

Lloyd George also displayed his concern – another very characteristic feature of the earlier part of his career – to ally himself with the dissenting tradition, and in particular with the more advanced pressure-groups on his side. In his speeches he was careful to locate his opposition to the war in a tradition running from Cromwell through Cobden and Bright to Gladstone, and one which viewed with anathema the imperialist ways of Disraeli, Lord Randolph Churchill and Joseph Chamberlain. In so doing he adopted a sage statesmanlike attitude to a rash folly. He told the Palmerston Club at Balliol College, Oxford, on 27 January 1900, 'We were rather fortunate ... that the follies of aggressive imperialism, which had dominated our statemanship for the last few years, had been brought home to us in a war with a small community in South Africa rather than in a struggle with a great European empire' (*Oxford Chronicle*, 3 February 1900). Yet, as usual, having committed himself to a course, he did not apologize for it but made his case with vigour and backed some of its most ardent advocates. In the case of the Boer War he joined the Stop-the-War Committee and also the League of Liberals against Aggression and Militarism (Fry, 1977, pp. 44, 51). Nevertheless, as a skilful politician, he also put out markers that he was willing to be conciliatory to those (including his constituents and those who differed within the Liberal Party) who did not take the same line.

In the earlier phase of the war there was more than an element of political, even physical, self-preservation in Lloyd George's willingness to appear conciliatory. The much-quoted passage from the *Western Mail* of 6 April 1900 states that Lloyd George is no Little Englander or pro-Boer but 'is of the school of Lord Rosebery on all other topics except the South African one' and 'even on this subject . . . is at one with the objects of the government, believing that the peace and prosperity of South Africa depend upon British rule being supreme in that part of the world'. It is presented by his biographers without the explanation that it was fed to the paper's London correspondent by Lloyd George in the hope of lessening uproar in his constituency when he spoke there the next week. Du Parcq, who produced his biography in close association with William George, even printed the comment that 'This paragraph must not be regarded as verbally inspired' (Du Parcq, (1912–13), vol. 2, p. 214). Yet this was very clearly the case, and the full 'London Letter' even includes 'I understand from Mr Lloyd George that he will make this point [of his attitude to South Africa] quite clear to his constituents, even though the prospect of being received by missiles after the speech is an imminent one.' Lloyd George and his supporters were right to worry. After his meeting in Bangor on 11 April he was hit over the head with a large stick. Similarly, he was well aware of the need to be cautious when he went into Joseph Chamberlain's territory of Birmingham on 18 December 1901. His prepared speech included praise of Lord Rosebery, the leading Liberal Imperialist. However, the expected rough reception turned out to be much worse than anticipated, and he was fortunate to leave Birmingham Town Hall alive.

But there was more to his conciliatoriness than short-term considerations. As so often with Lloyd George, his motives were multiple and are not to be explained in a simple way. During the war he was careful not to break all links with other elements in the Liberal Party. In it, as over the Education Bill, he did all he could to establish that while he was a formidable fighting politician, he was no ultra who would not compromise. He was hungry for office – and, as Martin Pugh has rightly commented, he was willing to back Rosebery as the more lively politician in preference to the old-style Radical, Sir Henry Campbell-Bannerman (Pugh, 1988, pp. 25–6). But this is not to say that he was soft on Rosebery at the height of the war. Thus, for example, in his speech at Balliol College, he commented cuttingly, 'Lord Rosebery would sharpen England's sword in order to make it more deadly. Let him rather purge the Empire's conscience, so as to make its statesmanship more upright.'

The Boer War had split the Liberal Party three ways by the middle of 1900. But once the set-piece battles had been won, the later guerrilla warfare phase, accompanied by the atrocious treatment of Boer women and children, pushed most of the Liberal Party back together again and turned the war into a political liability for the Government. In this phase Lloyd George came into his own. In the eyes of at least the Radical wing of the Liberal Party he was already the most heroic leading opponent of 'infamy' in South Africa.

Lloyd George followed his own deep-rooted nonconformist instincts, more than most modern historians allow. He did not merely play on the nonconformist interest. Just as his early attacks on aspects of the British monarchy owed much to an old-fashioned nonconformity (a Roundhead versus Cavalier outlook), so too this element was present in his attitude to the Boer War. An aspect of the real Lloyd George is revealed in some of his more bigoted remarks. Comments on the Boers such as, 'The only book was the Bible. Morning, noon and night it was the book they read, such as it was, and he would not expect German Jews to say much for it'; and 'Those men were the kind of men who were a simple type of the old Welsh Covenanters' (both made at his November 1899 Carmarthen meeting) say something about his outlook as well as that of his audience. In this he was a spokesperson for a part of British nonconformity (which was divided over the war), just as over Balfour's Education Act he spoke for a very large portion of it. The combination of the issues ensured his position as a Liberal politician of the front rank.

But the Boer War was also a major lesson to him in popular attitudes. He learned at first hand that the road to be travelled by an opponent of a nation's war is a very hard road indeed. Not only did he himself experience violence at several of his meetings but his family also suffered. His elder son Richard was bullied and had to be moved from a school in Dulwich to one in North Wales. His stand on the war adversely affected the family's law practice, and later Lloyd George said that had he not achieved office in December 1905 he might have been in serious financial straits, being £400 overdrawn at his bank (Riddell, 1933b, p. 157).

When he was faced with another war in 1914, the situation was

63

substantially different from that of 1899. For in 1914 the aggressor appeared to be Germany (or Austria), not Britain; and in 1914 Britain was dealing with a major power (or powers), not with small states. Moreover, by 1914 Lloyd George's earlier belief that with sufficient will a naval and political accord could be reached with Germany had been considerably undermined by his own experiences between 1908 and the outbreak of war. Nevertheless when war became imminent, Lloyd George did agonize over his response, joining the meetings of those ministers least willing to support war but − as Cameron Hazlehurst has observed − 'the evidence is clear that he did not dominate the group' (Hazlehurst, 1971, pp. 61−117).

In his *War Memoirs* Lloyd George understated his role in foreign policy before 1914. He conflated his experiences as the youngest member of the Cabinet with his later, more important position in decision-making as Chancellor of the Exchequer. Thus he wrote of the Cabinet as a whole, 'We were made to feel that, in these matters, we were reaching our hands towards the mysteries, and that we were too young in the priesthood to presume to enter into the sanctuary reserved for the elect' (Lloyd George, 1933, vol. 1, p. 78). This may well have been true of his early days as a Cabinet minister under Campbell-Bannerman. But, as Michael Fry has shown, Lloyd George participated in some decision-making from May 1908 when, as Chancellor of the Exchequer, he joined the Committee of Imperial Defence, and from early 1911 he was within the inner circle of ministerial decision-making. Again, contrary to the picture suggested by Lloyd George's *War Memoirs*, he and Edward Grey worked in harmony during much of Asquith's peacetime Governments. Lloyd George's later disparagement of Grey owed much to the First World War and even more to Grey's hostility to Lloyd George after 1918 (Fry, 1977, pp. 65−72, 126−7; Egerton, 1988, pp. 72−5). Indeed, before the war, at the time when Grey was warmly supporting the Land Campaign, Lloyd George said of him to Riddell, 'He is a kind fellow, the only a man I would serve under except Asquith' (Riddell, 1934, p. 171).

Lloyd George's attitude to foreign affairs before 1914 was not very different from Grey's. He recognized France to be Britain's necessary ally in continental Europe. In this he expressed himself to be part of a Radical tradition running from Charles James Fox to Gladstone. In his *War Memoirs* he dwelt on this, not hesitating to point out that, in contrast, 'Conservative opinion inclined to be more pro-German' and even that before 1905 'Lord Rosebery and his friends' had taken a

64

view which was more 'one of distrust of France and ill-concealed goodwill towards Germany' (Lloyd George, 1936, vol. 1, pp. 2–3). In fact, the main difference between him and Grey was the latter's lower expectations of German willingness to reach an agreement which would settle naval as well as other matters. But on several occasions Grey did try to negotiate with the German government, and at the time Lloyd George was not critical but was often appreciative of Grey's efforts. Undoubtedly, Lloyd George consistently took as his bottom line that he would not risk British naval superiority nor allow Germany to dominate the continent of Europe.

Yet there was a dichotomy in his approach. He was often very critical of the high public expenditure involved in maintaining British naval supremacy, especially when costs escalated to provide the new Dreadnoughts which rendered previous battleships near-obsolescent (Marder, 1961, pp. 56–70). Lloyd George's position as a leading Radical figure who had not only complained of inflated naval expenditure in the 1890s but, shortly before Campbell-Bannerman's Government was formed, had been calling for armaments reductions, and who had a lingering genuine wish for retrenchment whenever feasible, was reinforced both by his role as custodian of the public purse as Chancellor of the Exchequer and by his desire that higher priority should be given to expenditure on social measures. In the case of the army, Richard Haldane's reforms offered the solution of greater efficiency with reduced cost. But Admiral Fisher's reforms, with reliance on the Dreadnoughts, involved massive expenditure – especially when construction was related to Germany's programme.

So on several occasions Lloyd George clashed with the Admiralty over the naval programmes. He did so over the programmes brought forward in December 1907, 1908 and late 1910, on all these occasions with Churchill as one of his supporters. On 3 January 1909 he bluntly observed to Churchill, 'Frankly I believe the Admirals are procuring false information to frighten us' (R. S. Churchill, 1967, p. 516). Indeed, Fisher's political scheming to ensure that eight, not six, Dreadnoughts were built in the financial year 1909–10 was a precursor of the activities of French, Haig and Robertson during the First World War. From early in his time as a Cabinet minister Lloyd George realized that the surest and safest way to achieve reduced naval expenditure was to secure better relations with Germany. However, his own crude efforts at diplomacy when he visited Germany in the summer of 1908 did nothing to improve relations, though they did give him first-hand experience of the German government's 'distrust and suspicion' (Dockrill, 1971, pp. 7–9). In 1909 he did eventually accept the Admiralty's case for all eight Dreadnoughts, though he continued to look for an understanding with Germany.

Lloyd George later claimed in his *War Memoirs* that his awareness of Britain's unpreparedness for war, heightened by his visit to Germany in 1908, was one of his motivations in drawing up his secret coalition memorandum of 1910 (Lloyd George, 1936, vol. 1, pp. 20–1). As Bentley Gilbert has observed, this was a minor aspect of his document (Gilbert, 1987, p. 413). But there is strong evidence at the time of his concern that, just as Dreadnoughts had superseded other battleships, so new inventions might undermine the security that these battleships afforded, be the danger 'from the air or from under the waters'. He raised the issue of the dangers for Britain of air power both at a sub-committee of the Committee of Imperial Defence and publicly in interviews with the press in 1909 and also spoke strongly on the subject in the Commons in 1911, though by August 1912 he was resisting suggestions to spend additional sums on air power (Fry, 1977, pp. 121, 133, 165; Gollin, 1988, pp. 323–4).

In 1911 he came out strongly against Germany. The occasion for this was when the German government chose to ignore British representations while sending the gunboat *Panther* to Agadir in furtherance of its claims for territorial compensation from France for the latter's expanded role in Morocco. He gave Germany a firm warning at the Mansion House on 21 July during the course of the annual speech by the Chancellor of the Exchequer to City financiers. Lloyd George couched his words in the language of national unity, indeed, in the tone of his secret coalition proposals. He declared:

> if a situation were to be forced on us in which peace could only be preserved by the surrender of the great and benevolent position that Britain has won by centuries of hazard and achievement – by allowing Britain to be treated when her interests are vitally affected as if she were of no account in the Cabinet of Nations – then I say emphatically that peace at any price would be a humiliation, intolerable for a great country like ours to endure.
>
> National honour is no party question. The security of our great international trade is no party question. (*Manchester Guardian*, 22 July 1911)

Lloyd George's tough words – which he had shown beforehand to Asquith and Grey (and which the three of them had revised) –

caused a sensation. After this Lloyd George continued to adopt a belligerent stance until international relations improved in the autumn when a Franco-German understanding became likely. Sir Arthur Nicolson, the Permanent Under-Secretary at the Foreign Office, was not alone in recording during this period of international tension that both Lloyd George and Churchill were 'a little disappointed that war with Germany did not occur'. Nicolson further observed, 'I was struck with the determination of both of them not to permit Germany to assume the role of bully and at their belief that the present moment was an exceedingly favourable one to open hostilities' (Dockrill, 1971, p. 19; Fry, 1977, pp. 145–8).

Lloyd George's surprising role in the Agadir Crisis silenced Radical criticism for a while (Morris, 1972, pp. 242–6). But when opposition to Britain's role in the crisis focused on Grey, with demands for his resignation, Lloyd George made it known that if Grey were forced to resign, he would also resign. But by the start of 1912 Lloyd George was again not only speaking of doing a deal with Germany which might involve concessions in the Middle East, but was also reaffirming what was a major aspect of his attitude to Germany. In conversation with Rufus Isaacs, the Attorney-General, and Arthur Murray, Grey's Parliamentary Private Secretary, he said that Germany had to learn, 'Firstly that we intended to maintain the supremacy of our navy at whatever cost, and secondly that we did not propose to allow her to "bully" whomsoever she pleased on the continent of Europe.' In mid-February, when speaking privately of the possibility of helping France if she was threatened with German aggression, he observed that 'to bring the British public to fighting point it would be requisite that Germany should have passed into Belgium for the purpose of attacking France or should have crossed the French frontier' (Fry, 1977, pp. 150–2).

And yet over the next two years Lloyd George reverted to putting most emphasis on the need to try to reach an accord with Germany and so reduce naval expenditure. In so doing, he came to confront his former ally Churchill who, from October 1911, was First Lord of the Admiralty. Lloyd George accepted the Admiralty estimates prepared in late 1911 and late 1912 but strongly resisted the estimates that Churchill presented to the Cabinet in December 1913. Lloyd George did so partly because Churchill's demands amounted to an affront to the Radical wing of the Liberal Party, given Churchill's own belief, publicly proclaimed at the Guildhall in the City of London on 10 November 1913, that international tensions had lessened; and partly because he would be faced with meeting an £8–9 million deficit on the Budget if he met the increased naval demand (even if he rejected outright a £2 million education bid) in a period not far from a General Election. Hence Lloyd George and several of his Cabinet colleagues pressed Churchill to reduce his estimates in order to avoid new taxes (Wiemann, 1971, pp. 75–9).

In the ensuing public row Asquith backed Churchill, and Lloyd George had to give way. But though forced to propose new taxes, Lloyd George asserted, as in 1909, that they should fall hardest on the wealthy and that in the following year much of the benefit of such taxes would go to popular domestic expenditure: rating relief and education (Murray, 1990, pp. 60–72). This combination of electorally attractive Budget provisions in an election year combined with his re-emergence as a champion of the Radical side on armaments suggests that Lloyd George may have had in mind the safeguarding of his Radical credentials should the Liberals lose the next election and Asquith retire from the leadership. However, the outbreak of war in Europe ensured that a General Election did not take place in 1915. Though Lloyd George very clearly agonized over his position with the outbreak of a major European war in late July 1914, he was not vocal in threatening to resign as were others such as Sir John Simon. Indeed, there is no reason to differ from Michael Fry's verdict, 'In the final analysis ... he had sat too long with Asquith and Grey to walk away from responsibility and power' (Fry, 1977, p. 213). Having made his decision, Lloyd George as usual was to pursue his chosen course with great vigour. But unlike his domestic political campaigns, where a willingness to be conciliatory and even to do a deal with opponents often co-existed alongside the public displays of ardour, in fighting Germany and her allies Lloyd George only occasionally wavered from his determination to achieve outright victory.

As Chancellor of the Exchequer his prime role was to provide the financial means to carry on a major war. From early in the war he realized that it was likely to be long and costly. He warned a local government deputation in early September 1914 that 'as finance is going to play a very great part we must husband our resources ... The first hundred millions our enemies can stand just as well as we can, but the last they cannot' (Hazlehurst, 1971, p. 176). From his duty to provide the financial resources for the war, Lloyd George's almost hyperactive mind moved to the problems of supplying munitions and men.

But his first war work was to deal with the financial and commercial dislocations which occurred with the advent of a major European war. A large proportion of world trade was funded by short-term loans raised on the London money market. The outbreak of war threatened the ability of foreign borrowers to repay their debts, thereby undercutting confidence in the British financial institutions. It also seriously affected British businessmen's ability to transact their business with foreign customers. Similarly, much of the foreign side of stockbrokers' business was undermined, with resultant failures to pay for securities and falling share prices. Lloyd George necessarily became involved in a rescue operation. This involved the closure of the Stock Exchange on 31 July, the extension of the August Bank Holiday for three days, the raising of the Bank Rate to a record 10 per cent (from 3—4 per cent before 30 July) and a moratorium on bills of exchange (other than cheques), postponing payment for a month. In immersing himself in the ways of the money market Lloyd George won golden opinions from many for his ability to grasp quickly the essentials of the crisis. This was deserved, and it was indeed a high priority to end swiftly any chaos in the money markets. But in calming the situation he was certainly generous with Treasury finance — not least on 12 August when he underwrote the Bank of England's discounting at 5 per cent all approved bills drawn before 4 August, thereby guaranteeing the banks against bad debts and increasing their liquidity. At the same time as he was learning the ways of the money market (albeit in his sixth year as Chancellor), Lloyd George also adopted a state scheme of insurance against war risks for British shipping.

After these endeavours Lloyd George made his first major speech on the war at the Queen's Hall, London, on 19 September. Frances Stevenson later recalled:

> How we worked at that Queen's Hall speech! And how appre-
> hensive he was before it was delivered! With his Boer War
> record he realised how important it was. . . . People would have
> to be convinced of his sincerity. (F. Lloyd George, 1967,
> p. 75)

To a well-heeled, fashionable audience Lloyd George delivered a powerful speech which put the case for Britain to dedicate itself to the defeat of the German 'military caste'. In it he warned, 'It will be a long job; it will be a terrible war; but in the end we shall march through terror to triumph.' As at the time of the Agadir Crisis, he used the rhetoric of cross-party patriotism. In so doing he was not only stealing the Conservative Party's wartime political attire but putting himself at the forefront as a national leader. The sentiments in his final peroration could not have been bettered by any of the Conservative Party's ultra-patriots:

> We have been too comfortable and too indulgent, many, perhaps too selfish, and the stern hand of Fate has scourged us to an elevation where we can see the everlasting things that matter for a nation – the great peaks of Honour, Duty, Patriotism, and, clad in glittering white, the great pinnacle of Sacrifice pointing like a rugged finger to Heaven. (D. Lloyd George, 1915, pp. 11–14)

While he was careful to maintain an element of Radical credibility in identifying the enemy as the German ruling class ('The German people are under the heel of this military caste'), overall it was a speech intended to appeal to the Conservative part of the nation. Moreover, as John Grigg has pointed out, his eulogies to the spirit of sacrifice came ill to anyone aware of his earlier urgings (on 11 August) to his wife not to let his elder son volunteer too quickly, arguing that soon Russia would take on the German army ('I am not going to sacrifice my nice boy for that purpose') (Grigg, 1985, pp. 167–73).

From the autumn of 1914 Lloyd George became increasingly concerned about the supply of munitions. He saw to it that the War Office was not financially constrained, urging, 'The first interest of the taxpayer is that supplies should be secured.' So during the war Treasury control of expenditure gave precedence to the needs of the key wartime spending departments (Wrigley, 1990, p. 82). In spite of this, leading War Office officials remained reluctant to increase orders sufficiently. Lloyd George became impatient with their unwillingness to take necessary risks, such as giving orders beyond their established lists of contractors and their slowness to adapt production to the special needs of trench warfare in the muddy conditions of Flanders. He also became anxious that not enough munitions were being sent to help the Russian armies on the eastern frontiers of Germany and Austria-Hungary. Such concerns led Lloyd George from his role of organizer of wartime finances into major involvement with the provision of war supplies and strategy. He was an active member of both the Munitions Committee, set up on 12 October 1914, and the War Council, set up in late November 1914. These were Cabinet

70

Committees which overlooked the supply of munitions and broad issues of war policy.

In early 1915, building on his experience at the Board of Trade, Lloyd George became involved in negotiating agreements with the trade unions to facilitate higher output in war industries. By then the free labour market system had effectively collapsed in these sectors because so many men were volunteering for the armed forces and there was an escalating demand for war material. Moreover, the early patriotic willingness of working people to observe an industrial truce was undermined by the Government's expectation that they would assimilate the steeply rising cost of living. Strikes on Clydeside in February 1915 provided a warning both of the impact of this wartime inflation and of the need for the government to intervene in industrial relations.

In March the Cabinet delegated to Lloyd George the task of seeing the trade unions in order to 'try to get some sort of understanding with them before taking over the Armaments works'. This Lloyd George achieved in two sets of conferences held at the Treasury, the first between 17 and 19 March with representatives of the TUC, the General Federation of Trade Unions and the chief unions (other than the Amalgamated Society of Engineers, the miners and the railwaymen) involved in war work; and the second, on 25 March, with the Engineers who insisted on separate treatment. From these conferences Lloyd George emerged with a voluntary agreement that during the war there should be no strikes or lock-outs and that trade union restrictive practices should be lifted, while the state would ensure that any financial benefits accruing from this would go to the state, not to the employers, and that such practices would be restored at the end of the war (Wrigley, 1976, pp. 94–107). By the summer the failure of all parties to make the Treasury Agreement effective and the ever-growing need for greater war output led to this voluntary settlement being replaced by a statutory one, the Munitions of War Act of 2 July 1915.

By this time Asquith's purely Liberal Government had been superseded by a coalition government, still under his leadership, and Lloyd George had taken on the task of creating a Ministry of Munitions to meet more effectively the supply needs of the armed forces. The change of government was an inevitable outcome of such a war which was lasting well beyond a few months. The needs of this war created powerful pressure for changes in the economic organization of society

71

as well as in the machinery of government. It also put much political pressure on Bonar Law and the Unionist leadership, as under the political truce agreed in August 1914 they were inhibited in criticizing the conduct of the war and yet were excluded from office and responsibility.

The occasion for the change was the conjuncture in mid-May of the press's 'Shell Scandal' (substantially aided by Sir John French, who, fearing that Kitchener might replace him as Commander-in-Chief of the British Expeditionary Force, unduly emphasized the shortage of shells to deflect criticism from himself for the failure of recent offensives) and the impetuous departure from the Admiralty of Lord Fisher, the First Sea Lord (precipitated by his disagreement with Churchill over the sending of ships to Gallipoli). This double crisis gave Asquith good reasons to reconstitute his Government and continue in office, and thereby made it much easier to postpone the General Election which ordinarily had to be called before the end of the year (Pugh, 1974). Lloyd George's part in this change in the political complexion of the government was not that of a conspirator against Asquith (as suggested by Wilson, 1966, p. 52, and Koss, 1968), but simply that of a senior colleague who — with Bonar Law — saw the need for a coalition government in the circumstances of May 1915 and urged it on an acquiescent Asquith (Hazlehurst, 1971, pp. 232–69, 298–305).

Lloyd George's reputation as a dynamic minister while at Munitions has been upheld by recent writers (Adams, 1978; Wrigley, 1982; Grigg, 1985, pp. 256–75). However, there is greater recognition given now than formerly to what was achieved by Kitchener and the War Office in difficult circumstances before the Ministry of Munitions was created in May 1915. The War Office had employed businessmen before the much-heralded use of them by Lloyd George at Munitions, albeit on a smaller scale. Indeed, he took over some of these 'men of push and go' from the War Office. This was true of Eric Geddes, one of the foremost of his 'great improvisers', who had taken on particular tasks for the War Office while still employed by the North Eastern Railway (Grieves, 1989, pp. 10–14). But Lloyd George did foresee the scale of the need for munitions and he shook up the arrangements for procuring that supply. At Munitions he displayed his reliance on his intuition about people in making appointments, and then he gave those chosen the opportunity to succeed. He also showed his willingness to ride roughshod over civil service red tape. Whatever administrative drawbacks there were in his methods, Lloyd

George did ensure that there was a massive supply of munitions ready by the early summer of 1916 for what turned out to be the ill-fated major British offensive on the Somme. Moreover, his performance at Munitions confirmed his contemporaries' earlier impressions of him as a minister who was in command, not one who was run by his civil servants (Wrigley, 1982, pp. 40–6).

Lloyd George also built on his reputation as a skilful troubleshooter for the Government. In July 1915 he played the principal part in settling a major strike of coalminers in South Wales. In so doing he made substantial concessions; but he was a realist, knowing that continuous coal production was crucial and that all the miners could not be locked up for ignoring the newly enacted Munitions of War Act. (Such realism in these circumstances was to be repeated by Churchill's government during the Second World War.) On the Clyde, after persistent unrest, he took a very firm line in ensuring that the terms of the Munitions Act were carried out in the engineering works – and in March 1916 had nine leading militant shop stewards arrested and deported from the area (Wrigley, 1976, pp. 122–63).

These actions harmed such standing as he had with the more radical in the Labour movement, while earlier his inflated claims as to the evil impact on production of working men's drinking habits angered many firmly pro-war trade unionists. Thus, at the end of February 1915 Lloyd George told an audience at Bangor, 'Drink is doing more damage in the war than all the German submarines put together', and on 29 March 1915 he had told a delegation of employers, 'We are fighting Germany, Austria and drink; and, as far as I can see, the greatest of these three deadly foes is drink' (Lowe, 1971, pp. 103–4). While such remarks would have gone down well with some of his nonconformist and temperance supporters, they also marked part of his growing appeal to employers and to the Right in British politics.

This appeal stemmed from his undoubted determination to achieve victory. During 1915 and 1916 many who had found his politics repellant or had distrusted him came to admire his commitment to the war effort. When voluntary methods seemed to fail, Lloyd George accepted the need for compulsion. In 1915 and 1916 he moved markedly ahead of a substantial body of Liberal opinion over the issue of conscription. Kitchener's appeals to men to volunteer had created a mass army, but in so doing, men had left civilian work regardless of its importance to the war effort. Lloyd George was well aware of this and other problems in the labour market arising from his activities designed to procure a much greater supply of munitions. In June 1915 he aired the possibility of industrial conscription and thereafter sometimes threatened it as an alternative to other changes when negotiating with trade union leaders. But by September 1915 he was of the opinion that military conscription alone would be sufficient to secure order in the labour market. And from that August he was antagonizing many influential Liberals as the pre-eminent Liberal politician who saw conscription as desirable and inevitable.

After conscription had been introduced in stages in early 1916, Lloyd George justified his position to his constituents in a speech at Conway on 6 May. He commented:

> I am told that the fact that I supported it proves I am no longer a Liberal. Well, there must be a good many Liberals in the same plight, because the other night barely one-tenth of the Liberal Party voted against it. ... After all ... great democracies in peril have always had to resort to compulsion to save themselves. ... It is purely ... a means of organising the strength and virility of a nation to save itself from oppression, and that is why, as a Liberal fighting the battle of liberty in Europe, I have no shame in declaring for compulsory enlistment as I would for compulsory taxes or for compulsory education, or ... for compulsory insurance.

He went on to defend his overall position on the war. In so doing he expressed what was truly the essence of his wartime politics. He declared:

> I hate war. ... But you either make war or you don't. It is the business of statesmen to strain every nerve to keep a nation out of war, but once they are in it, it is also their business to wage it with all their might ... I want this to be the last, and it won't be unless this war is effectively managed by us. A badly conducted war means a bad peace, and a bad peace means no peace at all. That is why I have urged that this war should be conducted with determination. (Lloyd George, 1918, pp. 14, 17–18)

Yet while he was a very vigorous advocate of a maximum commitment to the war effort, he was no uncritical admirer of the military High Command. He persistently favoured 'Easterner' strategies – feeling that it was highly desirable to develop a front in Salonika and also one in Syria. During 1915 he advocated action in Salonika by Britain and France as a way to prevent the defeat of Serbia, to bring

74

Romania and Greece into the war on the Allies' side and to help Russia. He was much attached to the possibility of defeating Germany's weaker partners — Austria and Turkey — thereby, as he put it, 'bringing Germany down by the process of knocking the props under her'. In expecting that the arrival of a small Anglo-French force would have a major impact on Balkan opinion, Lloyd George was being unduly optimistic (Woodward, 1983, pp. 27–45, 59–65; French, 1986, pp. 66–8). But in retrospect his policy had the political advantages of identifying him firmly with neither the ill-fated Gallipoli campaign which engulfed Churchill nor (in due course, when the battle of post-war memoirs got underway) with a war policy confined to endless bloody offensives on the Western Front. His espousal of Salonika as a means of assisting Serbia also helped (along with his record at Munitions and his views on conscription) to bring him closer to such influential figures on the Right as Sir Edward Carson and Lord Milner.

Yet while Lloyd George was unwilling to support unreservedly and exclusively the policy of offensives on the Western Front in the manner which Generals Haig and Robertson wished, they did recognize his dynamism and full-blooded commitment to victory. For 1915 and 1916 there is much to be said for David French's judgement:

> The real division between British policy-makers was not between 'Easterners' and 'Westerners'. It was between those like Reginald McKenna ... who argued that Britain could best assist her allies by limiting the size of her own army and giving them money and equipment, and those like Robertson and Lloyd George who by the summer of 1915 championed the cause of a large conscript army as the only way of demonstrating to France and Russia that Britain had not abandoned them. (French, 1988(a), p. 24)

Although there were very substantial tensions between Lloyd George and the generals, and these were to be acute at times during 1916, Lloyd George was seen by them as a lesser evil than Asquith and his associates. Sir Henry Wilson put this bluntly to Lloyd George on 26 November 1916, telling him, 'The present government stank in the nostrils of the whole army ... if he was to break away and raise the standard of victory he would have a unanimous army behind him' (Guinn, 1965, p. 180).

Lloyd George's relations with Asquith had taken a turn for the worse from the late summer of 1915. Asquith was well aware that Lloyd George was meeting with their Unionist ministerial colleagues to discuss conscription. Such activities, along with Lloyd George's publicly expressed views on that subject, inevitably created tension with his Liberal colleagues (Taylor, 1971(b), pp. 56–61). As well as differing from Asquith over the need for a speedy introduction of conscription, Lloyd George had become increasingly unhappy about the higher direction of the war. Shortly after Carson resigned on 12 October 1915 over the failure to help Serbia, Lloyd George told Riddell, 'The reorganisation of the Cabinet is what is wanted; we are sure to be beaten under the present regime' (23 October 1916, in Riddell, 1933(a), p. 128).

Although Lloyd George pressed hard and Asquith gave some ground, the end result was a characteristic Asquithian fudge which pleased nobody. Asquith resisted Lloyd George's demands for a smaller Cabinet but did agree to a small War Committee. When he proposed to put Kitchener on it, Bonar Law and Lloyd George threatened to resign if Kitchener were not excluded and, indeed, removed from the War Office. Asquith then 'devised a crafty way of getting rid of K' (as Frances Stevenson aptly put it), by sending him to assess the military situation in the eastern Mediterranean and the Dardanelles. Asquith also reduced the responsibilities of the Secretary of State for War. As for the War Committee, Asquith backtracked over its membership – adding his associate McKenna even though he himself had earlier explicitly excluded him. In adding the minister most hostile to Lloyd George and one who had major doubts about Britain's economic capacity to wage all-out war for any length of time, Asquith was ensuring that there would be substantial friction on the Committee. Frances Stevenson observed in her diary, 'it seems to me that his appointment will destroy the usefulness of it to a large extent' – a view most probably shared by Lloyd George (Taylor, 1971(b), pp. 72–3).

Thereafter, Lloyd George's relationship with Asquith waxed and waned by turns. By the end of 1915 Lloyd George had quite clearly marked out his own distinctive position from that of Asquith. He had also successfully pushed Asquith over various policies, including changing the format of civilian control of the war, maintaining the Anglo-French force in Salonika and conscription. He underlined his semi-detached position within Asquith's government in a major speech on munitions production given in the House of Commons on 20 December 1915. In it his warning – 'I beg employers and workmen not to have "Too Late" inscribed upon the portals of their workshops' — provided very thin concealment indeed for what was intended — and taken — as powerful criticism of the Asquith Government's management of the war. He declared:

Too late in moving here! Too late in arriving there! Too late in coming to this decision! Too late in starting with enterprises! Too late in preparing! In this war the footsteps of the Allied forces have been dogged by the mocking spectre of 'Too Late'; and unless we quicken our movements damnation will fall on the sacred cause for which so much gallant blood has flowed. (Lloyd George, 1918, p. 7)

Lloyd George thus distanced himself from Britain's relative lack of success in the war and also made it clear that he was the leading alternative Liberal committed to the war should Asquith trip and fall — or be pushed.

However, when it came to the final political crisis over the introduction of conscription in April 1916, Lloyd George was firm but took pains to make it clear that he was not out to oust Asquith. He took the view that Asquith alone could get the measure through the House of Commons. In helping Asquith, Frances Stevenson noted, Lloyd George felt that 'the section of Liberals who were angry with [him] before and talked about "plots" and "intrigues" will realise that he is not out to wreck the government and must give him credit for having done his best to preserve unity in the Cabinet' (Taylor, 1971(b), pp. 106–8). But Lloyd George was looking ahead to the political situation on Asquith's fall, which he was convinced was only a matter of time.

However, the political situation and Lloyd George's personal position were much changed on 25 April by the Easter Rising in Dublin and on 5 June 1916 by the drowning of Kitchener, who had again been despatched overseas by Asquith, this time to Russia. In asking Lloyd George to try to achieve an Irish settlement in the aftermath of the Rising, Asquith probably saved Lloyd George from drowning, for he had seriously contemplated accompanying Kitchener to Russia. In taking on the Irish negotiations Lloyd George was faced with an issue which could break his career. But there was also much in Riddell's comment of the time, 'This appointment gives you the reversion of the premiership. Mr A. and the Cabinet have admitted your position' (Riddell, 1933(a), p. 184).

Lloyd George did enhance his reputation as a negotiator. He

secured agreement with the leaders of the Irish Nationalists and the Ulster Unionists that Ireland other than the Ulster provinces would have Home Rule immediately, while Ulster would be excluded and so remain part of the United Kingdom. But with characteristic skilful ambiguity in negotiations, Lloyd George avoided clarifying whether such exclusion was for the duration of the war or was to be permanent. When the deal reached the Cabinet, Lansdowne, Selborne and Long revolted; and Asquith and Lloyd George failed to insist on it, even though more important Unionists – Bonar Law, Balfour and F. E. Smith – backed Lloyd George's settlement. The scale of the concessions made and the failure, nevertheless, to achieve anything helped to ruin the Irish Nationalists politically and destroyed their trust in Lloyd George or Asquith. John Grigg has delivered the verdict that their failure to force such a deal through in the face of 'the susceptibilities of such relatively unimportant figures, when the acknowledged leaders of Unionism were supporting it, was an appalling failure of judgement and nerve' (Grigg, 1985, p. 353).

Perhaps on Lloyd George's part it was another sign that his prime concern, alongside winning the war, was to be in the best possible political position for the succession when Asquith finally crumbled. He was anxious not to be manoeuvred into resigning on an issue to suit Asquith and his associates. Frances Stevenson, after speaking with him on the subject, noted that if he resigned 'the Asquithites might be able to exclude him from the Cabinet altogether and thus rob him of a great part of his power ... Whereas if D. remains where his is, he retains his power, and when the government falls, he will be as powerful as any of them' (Taylor, 1971(b), p. 111). Moreover, Lloyd George had alienated much Liberal support and courted the Unionists in the previous 12 months. He was not likely to risk that for the Irish Nationalists, who had declined to join the wartime coalition government.

Similar considerations affected his decision to accept the War Office. He wondered if he could afford to take it on the reduced terms that had latterly been imposed on Kitchener. On the other hand, resignation from the Government over the direction of the war was politically more attractive than allowing someone else to accept that office while he continued in the now more routine task of Minister of Munitions. But to resign would weaken his position as the militaristic Crown Prince. Hence, after consulting such associates as Carson, Lloyd George did accept the Secretaryship of State for War, without securing a commitment for the restoration to that office of powers that had been transferred from Kitchener to Robertson (as Chief of the General Staff).

Lloyd George's time at the War Office, from 7 July 1916, was not one of conspicuous achievement. But neither was it politically disastrous. His main success was to get Haig to agree to the appointment of Sir Eric Geddes, the businessman from the North Eastern Railway, to remedy the transport blockages behind the front lines which had been exposed acutely during the Battle of the Somme. In September 1916 he went one step further, enraging the military establishment by appointing Geddes as Director General of Military Railways and giving him the honorary rank of major-general (Grieves, 1989, pp. 29–35). As for what should have been his major role, Peter Rowland has given the verdict, 'So far as the conduct of the war was concerned, Lloyd George might as well have been invisible. He gave advice which nobody took and wrote letters which nobody read' (Rowland, 1975, p. 343).

His period as Secretary of State for War nearly coincided with the ill-fated Battle of the Somme, which began on 1 July and ended on 18 November 1916. Lloyd George approved of the early weeks of that offensive, noting that it was drawing the efforts of much of the German Army, thereby lessening the pressure on the French at Verdun and easing the way for the Russian offensive against the Austrians. But by September Lloyd George was again more concerned to take action in the Balkans, this time to help Romania which had entered the war on 27 August, and in Arabia against the Turks. His disillusionment with the Somme offensive was fortified by a visit to the Western Front in mid-September. Thereafter he was to comment to Hankey that it was 'a bloody and disastrous failure' and to Sir Max Aitken (soon to be Lord Beaverbrook), 'I am the butcher's boy who leads the animals to be slaughtered – when I have delivered the men my task in the war is over' (Woodward, 1983, pp. 102–13).

Much of the latter half of Lloyd George's time at the War Office was marked by his efforts to outwit Robertson and Haig on major matters of policy and by their equally, or more, effective political manoeuvring to neutralize his role. Both he and they were skilful users of the press to further their causes. Lloyd George, with good cause, feared that unless some new initiative was taken to assist Romania it would be crushed just as Serbia had been earlier. In pressing his case he inevitably ran into Robertson's objections to diverting resources from the Western Front. Asquith backed Robertson. Lloyd George urged again a small War Council with real powers as a means of effectively controlling the war effort and of controlling Robertson. As David Woodward has observed, in demanding the War Council, 'it was Robertson and the military policy he represented – not Asquith – whom Lloyd George hoped to overthrow' (Woodward, 1983, p. 121). Yet the demand for an effective small War Council was the occasion for Asquith's fall on 5 December and Lloyd George's accession to the premiership on 7 December 1916. But in itself it was a reasonable demand, likely to increase the efficiency of the running of the war. It was an idea of which Sir Maurice Hankey, the Secretary of the War Council and its successor bodies, approved; and, indeed it probably originated with him (Hankey, 1961, pp. 562–4).

Historians have long discounted the old view that Asquith fell because Lloyd George conspired (Hazlehurst, 1968, 1976; Lowe, 1971, pp. 124–31; and the latest reassessment, Fry, 1988, p. 610). In rebutting the darker pictures of Lloyd George, painted by Thomson (1965) and earlier by Asquith's official biographers (Spender and Asquith, 1932, vol. 2, p. 273) Hazlehurst argued, 'There is abundant testimony that Lloyd George was not anxious to assume the supreme responsibility of the premiership' (Hazlehurst, 1968, p. 157). There is a strong case for judging that Lloyd George's objective in late 1916 was to secure a firmer direction of the war and not to end Asquith's premiership. But nevertheless Lloyd George had long been manoeuvring to ensure that he was the Crown Prince whenever Asquith's position collapsed – and he undoubtedly saw the need for such a change in the control of the direction of the war as being more vital than maintaining Asquith in power ('unity without action is nothing but futile carnage', as he put it in his resignation letter to Asquith on 5 December).

Lloyd George had been consistent, and even politically courageous, in his advocacy of a more-determined and better-directed war effort. This is illustrated both by his advocacy of conscription and by his manoeuvres to achieve greater civilian control of the generals. With the former he was liable to alienate many Liberals; with the latter he was likely to alienate the Right. But overall there could be no doubting his commitment to victory. This he underlined when he gave an American journalist an interview on 26 September 1916 in which he vigorously rebutted the peace soundings of President Wilson and others. In it he asserted, 'there will be no quitters among the Allies', and declared that 'The fight must be to a finish – to a knock-out.' Lloyd George's policy of the 'knock-out blow' marked out his position as unequivocally as had his 'Too Late' speech ten months earlier. That his warning over Romania proved all too true, with Romania crumbling from late October and being effectively defeated by 6 December, did him no harm in the eyes of Carson and the Right. At the same time, Bonar Law's difficulties in maintaining control over his dissatisfied backbenchers destabilized his support for the various political compromises that Asquith had stitched together and which were embodied in his coalition government, making it more probable that he would accept a new political arrangement.

But while his ends were eminently defensible, as so often with Lloyd George, his means of achieving them were shrouded in all manner of manoeuvring with prominent newspapermen as well as politicians. But Lloyd George did not create the widespread dissatisfaction in the press with Asquith's conduct of the war. While the Conservative press's complaints of 'weak methods and weak men' were the norm, by late November, as Professor McEwen has shown (McEwen, 1978), there was evident diminishing confidence in Asquith's Government among the Liberal press. Thus, for example, on 29 November J. A. Spender, editor of the *Westminster Gazette* and one of Asquith's most stalwart journalistic supporters, complained of 'an appearance of delay and indecision which ... makes an unhappy impression'. As Lloyd George braced himself for a likely showdown with Asquith, he saw potential political allies (including even leading Irish Nationalists) and massaged the press to ensure that his demand for a small War Committee was favourably presented by it. His efforts, on top of the existing disquiet in the press over the conduct of the war, were sufficient to ensure that Asquith was not able to fudge and evade a clear commitment to real change as he had done in October 1915. Lloyd George's manocuvres were also intended to ensure that he had a good foundation of political support whatever the outcome of the confrontation over a small War Committee. If he lost, he was not going to retire to a personal library, in the manner of Lord Morley or John Burns.

As for Asquith, there have been a range of explanations for his conduct. Cameron Hazlehurst has argued, 'He removed himself. He could not have been dislodged by the forces initially ranged against him' (Hazlehurst, 1976). If so, there remains the question of whether Asquith 'momentarily lost his nerve' (Hazlehurst, 1968, p. 156; 1970, p. 530) or whether his resignation was a cunning move to show his indispensability, which misfired as several historians have argued (for example, Lowe, 1971, p. 129; Bourne, 1989, p. 126). Asquith undoubtedly was tired and had been demoralized for a while in the autumn, following the death of his son Raymond during an offensive on the Somme on 15 September 1916. He had been pushed frequently enough by Lloyd George and the Unionists over conscription and other issues to be unwilling to suffer further loss of face, as seemed inevitable if he compromised on the formation of a small War Committee, given the newspaper reports. But his resignation can also reasonably be seen as a realistic assessment that, after several days of manoeuvring in a political crisis, the game was up. Conservative backbench unrest had been destabilizing Bonar Law's position and making him more amenable to acting with Lloyd George and Carson. The dithering over the proposed small War Committee set off a train of circumstances which united those hostile to Asquith with those who were merely dissatisfied with the jaded leadership now being given by him. Trevor Wilson has argued that 'it was quite evident by the evening of 5 December 1916 that Asquith no longer had the numbers in Parliament to remain Prime Minister' (Wilson, 1986, p. 422). And indeed, A. J. P. Taylor argued long ago:

> The first Coalition was made against parliamentary discontent, to silence and thwart it; the second Coalition owed its existence to parliamentary discontent, which dictated to Bonar Law as much as against Asquith. (Taylor, 1959, p. 87)

As Asquith did not call a vote of confidence in the Commons, one cannot know whether he still maintained the confidence of a majority of MPs. But it is very clear that in Parliament support was ebbing away from him.

Lloyd George took on the premiership with genuine hesitation after Bonar Law had declined the task. He had expressed his doubts in mid-November to Frances Stevenson, after talking with Carson and Aitken. She noted, 'Had they asked him, some months ago, he said, it would have been a different matter: but now, he would simply get blamed for losing the war, and have the negotiating of an unfavourable peace.' Moreover he dwelt on the distrust he would suffer from both the Unionists and the Liberals (Taylor, 1971(b), p. 123). Lloyd George undoubtedly had been willing to continue to serve under Asquith in a suitably reconstituted coalition government. With Asquith refusing to serve under Balfour, Bonar Law or Lloyd George, Lloyd George set about constructing his Government from the Unionists, those Liberals who supported him and Labour. He needed all his charm and charisma to secure the support of distrustful Tory grandees and Labour leaders. Of his meeting with Labour, Frances Stevenson noted:

> Everything depended on it, and D was at his craftiest. They asked him awkward questions, and he put them off with chaff. The majority of them came there sulky, hostile, and they went away laughing and friendly.   (Taylor, 1971(b), p. 134)

But in a sense the decision had been made earlier, on 4 December, when Arthur Henderson had made it clear to a meeting of Liberal ministers that Labour's priority was to support any prime minister who got on with winning the war and not just to back Asquith personally.

In taking the premiership Lloyd George, of course, had the opportunity to create the more efficient structure of government which he had been demanding since 1915. Instead of two alternative sources of power in the direction of the war – the Cabinet and the War Committee – Lloyd George substituted one supreme small body: the War Cabinet. Four of the five members of the War Cabinet (Bonar Law was the exception, being Leader of the House of Commons and Chancellor of the Exchequer) were largely un-encumbered by heavy administrative and Parliamentary duties; this was in striking contrast to the 11 members of the War Committee, and hence they were able to concentrate fully on the war. Hankey (who was the War Cabinet's secretary) later observed of it, 'The system was essentially flexible, and subjects were redistributed to meet changing circumstances.' He added, 'The War Cabinet therefore became in effect the supreme control ... with the Prime Minister as the dominating and directing force', with its system of delegation providing 'a safeguard against congestion of business' (Hankey, 1945, pp. 40–1). Lloyd George's War Cabinet was administratively more effective and it gave the premier great power.

Lloyd George's hold over the central government machine was further strengthened by his establishment of a special prime ministerial secretariat which acted as 'an administrative intelligence department' for him. This secretariat, located in temporary offices in the gardens of 10 and 11 Downing Street (hence known as the 'garden suburb'), provided Lloyd George with detailed background information before decisions were taken and thereafter helped to monitor how effectively such decisions were carried out (Turner, 1980, pp. 1, 5). It was headed by Professor W. G. S. Adams, who had served Lloyd George very well at the Ministry of Munitions and who – as 'a model of

83

urbane and tactful consideration' (as Thomas Jones put it) – played a very important role in lessening friction between it and Whitehall (Sir Joseph Davies, 1951, p. xx).

Lloyd George also created new ministries, beginning with Food, Labour, Pensions and Shipping. In 1917 he added National Service and Reconstruction. The initial batch of new ministries were in areas of working-class sensitivity, and Lloyd George made much of his intention to set them up when he saw a deputation from the Parliamentary Labour Party and the Labour Party's National Executive on 7 December 1916, at the time when Labour was considering whether to support his government. More than this, at that meeting he declared that not only would Labour have a place in his small War Cabinet but that in his opinion both the Ministry of Labour and the Ministry of Pensions 'should be under the control of a Labour representative' (Lloyd George, 1933, vol. 2, pp. 997–8). But for other new ministries and senior posts Lloyd George turned to outside 'experts' and businessmen. Thus he brought in men such a H. A. L. Fisher, the Vice-Chancellor of Sheffield University, to the Board of Education; R. E. Prothero, who had been agent of the Duke of Bedford's estates, to the Ministry of Agriculture; Sir Joseph Maclay, a Glasgow shipping magnate, to be Shipping Director; Lord Devonport, who had made his fortune in food distribution, to be Food Controller; Lord Cowdray, a major civil engineering contractor, to chair the Air Board; Sir Albert Stanley, a director of the London Underground Railway, to the Board of Trade; and Lord Rhondda, a substantial businessman and financier, to the Local Government Board.

Writers have differed as to how dramatic were these changes to the machinery of government. Professor Trevor Wilson in his major study of the First World War has suggested that it is too simplistic to suggest that these changes are evidence that Lloyd George's Government 'possessed a much stronger commitment to the philosophy of state control at the expense of individual freedom'. He suggests that though this may be true, it needs to be qualified by recognizing that it may have been 'less the change of government than the changing nature of the conflict that determined these new forms of action' (Wilson, 1986, p. 533).

Similarly, Dr Bourne in his astute study of the First World War has argued that there was 'an underlying continuity between his government and its wartime predecessors', and that 'The real differences between Lloyd George's government and Asquith's were of style rather than substance' (Bourne, 1989, p. 130). That there was continuity was natural, but it is taking revisionism too far to see the changes as purely 'style'. Hankey himself, late in the Second World War, observed of the First, 'We owed much to Mr Asquith's solid spade-work, but in each sphere the system reached its maximum efficiency under the initiative of one man — David Lloyd George.' Having paid tribute to such continuity, Hankey went on to state:

> He is undoubtedly the founder of our modern system of Government Control in War, and for my part, as a witness and official recorder of these events, I wish to place on record my conviction that the man who won the war was David Lloyd George. (Hankey, 1945, pp. 49–50)

This view, so firmly expressed by Hankey, has long been subject to much revision. John Turner, indeed, has argued that 'the essential difference . . . was political, not administrative: Lloyd George, unlike Asquith, was able to rid himself of significant internal opposition.' But to depict the organizational changes as stemming from Lloyd George acting 'to dress up a purge as an administrative revolution' is also to go too far in reassessing them. But otherwise Turner is right, in reappraising the administrative changes, to find that the new War Cabinet system, for all its improvements, did not provide anything like an entirely satisfactory means of drawing on departmental knowledge or resolving differences within Whitehall (Turner, 1982, pp. 63, 75–8).

Lloyd George's own immense capacity for work helped to make this new wartime system of government effective. Contrary to popular opinion then and subsequently, Lloyd George was, as Hankey has testified:

> an omnivorous reader. He usually woke early. His official papers were placed by his bedside overnight, and at an early hour he would apply himself to them. . . . By breakfast time the Prime Minister had mastered the contents of a mass of official and unofficial documents, and had skimmed through the whole of the London Press as well as a good many provincial newspapers, especially the Welsh ones, and was ready to begin — what was really his main fount of knowledge — sucking the brains of the best men he could get on every subject. (Hankey, 1961, pp. 575–6)

Though Lloyd George often infuriated tidy administrative minds by the way he rode roughshod over agendas, repeatedly postponed decisions on lesser matters and generally approached matters in an intuitive rather than a systematic manner, men such as Hankey nevertheless saw his role as decisive.

Whether or not he deserved to be known as 'The Man Who Won the War' is a contentious matter, but there is no doubt that a wide range of contemporaries were very impressed by his record as wartime prime minister. For example, F. S. Oliver, a close associate of Lord Milner, commented in a letter to Hankey on Armistice Day 1918:

> England has never in her whole history had a war minister whom I should put above him. ... Of course great men are built to scale, i.e. their faults as well as their virtues are big. But I have seen the little man in intimacy – at the worst crises of our fortunes. I have seen him well and ill. But I have never seen him anything but courageous. His enterprising imagination has never been numbed or paralysed. And he has always had vision. (Hankey Papers 4/10/30)

Lloyd George's position as prime minister owed nearly everything to his personal attributes and relatively little to party. For he was a prime minister who was not leader of his party and who was dependent on the support of the Conservative and Labour parties as well as a portion of the Liberals. His position put a premium on his performing well. On 16 September 1918, when in fact Lloyd George was suffering from influenza, Lord Esher commented after Lloyd George had given a below-par speech, that it looked 'as if he was conscious of inability to contend with the difficulties of his task'. He added that 'the little man should not give the impression of temperamental weakening. His power rests entirely on the sense of confidence inspired by strength of character and purpose' (Hankey Papers 4/10/22).

Hence, though Lloyd George was in a powerful position within his newly adapted machinery of government, there was always fragility in his political position while premier. For all of Lloyd George's subsequent talk that the positions in his Government were filled on merit, not on party grounds, the membership of his War Cabinet reflected the political realities of the start of his premiership. Two of the four members (the Prime Minister being the fifth), Bonar Law and Henderson, were the leaders of the Conservative and Labour parties. The inclusion of Milner and Curzon added two major imperial figures: Milner, who had been a Liberal Unionist, was a hero of many Social Imperialists on the Right while Curzon was a capable figure of traditional Toryism. For a period (July 1917–January 1918) Sir Edward Carson was also a member. His importance then stemmed from the widespread support he commanded among many Conservative backbenchers, making him at times during the war effectively the leader of parliamentary opposition to the Government, rather than from his role as Protestant Ulster's spokesperson. Another later addition to the War Cabinet (from June 1917) was Jan Christian Smuts, the South African Minister of Defence and former Boer general. His inclusion stemmed from Lloyd George's effort to emphasize the Empire's role, and in particular Lloyd George's establishment of the Imperial War Cabinet in London in March 1917.

Although Lloyd George's position was strong in controlling the supreme direction of the war, he felt politically insecure at least until well into 1918. This is in spite of the view of contemporaries and later commentators that his premiership was one of 'unalloyed dictatorship' or, as Arthur Henderson observed of 1917, 'L. G. was the War Cabinet and nobody else really counted.' As a result of his uncertain political position Lloyd George's premiership was marked by his need to create for himself bodies of political support – during the war, the Coalition Liberal organization, and after it, various moves towards the formation of a Centre Party (Morgan, 1970).

For all his changes in the higher direction of the war, Lloyd George even as Prime Minister found it politically difficult to control the policies of his top generals. In 1917 and 1918 he was faced with the political reality that the removal of Sir Douglas Haig as Commander-in-Chief would lead to major troubles with influential sections of the Conservative Party and also with the King. It was only with great care – and no small measure of cunning – that he managed to replace Sir William Robertson as Chief of the Imperial General Staff in February 1918 and Lord Derby, who had become a mouthpiece for the generals, as Secretary of State for War in April 1918. Their successors, Sir Henry Wilson and Lord Milner, were much more amenable.

During 1917 and into the summer of 1918 Lloyd George had little or no confidence that major attacks by the British Army on the Western Front would break the German Army. Moreover he had come to dislike and distrust Haig. In early 1917, in spite of his usual agnosticism concerning offensives on the Western Front, he was so attracted by the charisma of the French general, Robert Nivelle and by his promise of quick results that he supported a French-led offensive. At the same time he overreached himself in his efforts to subordinate Haig and Robertson to political control. At an Anglo-French conference at Calais in late February 1917 Lloyd George pressed hard to give Nivelle supreme command over the British as well as the French Army. In getting Haig and Robertson to sign a compromise agreement which still gave Nivelle great authority over the British Army, Lloyd George exercised all his dubious skills of negotiating – including, notably, a spurious claim to have the full authority of the War Cabinet for his initial proposals (Woodward, 1983, pp. 145–9). To put the now large British Army under the French was a dangerous political move, given his reliance on Conservative support. It also discredited his military judgement when Nivelle's offensive failed, thereby ensuring that it was politically impossible for him to prevent Haig undertaking his preferred plan: to attack the Passchendaele Ridge in order to reach the plains and the Belgian coast beyond.

Lloyd George was genuinely appalled by the loss of life involved in such British offensives as those at the Somme and Passchendaele. He was also concerned at the effect these had on Britain's overall labour resources which were being stretched near to the limit. Haig appeared to have no comprehension that Britain's manpower, like other resources, was finite. Lloyd George also had his eye on Britain's role in the post-war settlement. He realized that her position at the peace conference would be much stronger if her military strength remained largely intact.

However, Lloyd George's political position prevented him from taking the straightforward course of sacking Haig as a commander in whom he lacked confidence. Though, it has to be added, there was also a problem for Lloyd George in finding a replacement who was both militarily credible and likely to be more amenable to his views. As he admitted in his *War Memoirs* in the midst of a sustained and severe attack on Haig, 'There was no conspicuous officer in the Army who seemed to be better qualified for the Highest Command than Haig' (Lloyd George, 1936, vol. 6, p. 3424). So Lloyd George manoeuvred to try to lessen Haig's powers of discretion to launch and then continue costly offensives. After his efforts at Calais, in June Lloyd George created in effect an inner War Cabinet (the War Policy Committee) and then in November 1917 established the supreme War Council at Versailles as part of his efforts to curb his own generals. In creating the latter he was assisted by the very costly failure of Haig's Passchendaele campaign and by the Central Powers' successful offensive at Caporetto against Italy (a front for which

Lloyd George had unsuccessfully sought reinforcements). On both issues Lloyd George could have asserted himself, stopping the Passchendaele offensive sooner and insisting on troops being sent to Italy. Perhaps the fact that he did not do so was a sign not only of political weakness but also of him acting on the principle of giving Haig enough rope to hang himself.

If Lloyd George's manoeuvres against his own generals were unseemly and even outrageous, the same must be said about Haig and Robertson. They exerted all the influence they had to check Lloyd George and his colleagues – unashamedly and often brazenly using the King, the press and Conservative MPs. This included providing the military journalist Colonel Charles Repington with top secret manpower information to use in the right-wing *Morning Post* against the Government (Woodward, 1983, pp. 246–7). The generals also repeatedly arranged for deliberately misleading appraisals to be presented to the Government to ensure that their views prevailed. A notably outrageous example occurred when Allenby, at Robertson's prompting, in October 1917 supplied grossly inflated estimates of the forces that he would need to advance on Jerusalem (Woodward, 1983, pp. 199, 206, 211, 231). But in manipulating figures and in one-sided presentation of material, the generals met their equal in Lloyd George.

The success of Ludendorff's offensive of 21 March 1918, which was aimed at dividing the British and French Armies, provided a major occasion for further recriminations between Lloyd George and the generals as each side tried to fix the blame for the reverse on the other. When Major-General Sir Frederick Maurice, who had been until recently Director of Military Operations, took to the *Morning Post* on 6 May 1918 a letter in which he challenged the truthfulness of Lloyd George in two statements and Bonar Law in one, concerning the adequacy of manpower on the Western Front, he created a political sensation and put Lloyd George's Government in jeopardy. Lloyd George – probably wrongly – suspected that Haig and Robertson were behind the move and intended the overthrow of the Government. Lloyd George shrewdly made Asquith's demand for a select committee to examine Maurice's charges into an issue of confidence. Maurice was wrong over Bonar Law and one of Lloyd George's errors was to do with a minor matter. As for the main set of incorrect figures, Lloyd George in the ensuing parliamentary debate made much of the fact that they had been supplied by Maurice's own department and suppressed a later correction from that department.

He offered the Commons the stark choice of backing him or reinstating Asquith as Prime Minister. He won his vote of confidence by 293 to 106 votes (Woodward, 1983, pp. 292–304). Thereafter, during the war Lloyd George's political position was secure.

The success of the German offensive of March 1918 also provided the occasion for the appointment of General Ferdinand Foch as General-in-Chief of the Allied Forces. Lloyd George, mindful of Britain's shortage of manpower, remained opposed to further great offensives on the Western Front, at least in 1918. However, fortunately for him, Lloyd George did not impede Haig's offensive of 8 August 1918 which began the successful Allied advance to the German frontier.

Lloyd George was not only unhappy with Britain's military leadership, he also lacked confidence in Sir John Jellicoe, First Sea Lord. He deplored his cautious and pessimistic nature. Lloyd George later observed of the Admiralty after the inconclusive Battle of Jutland (April 1916) that it was enveloped in an 'atmosphere of crouching nervousness, even before the Germans had launched more than a few of their latest specimens of submarine cruisers' (Lloyd George, 1934, vol. 3, p. 1135).

Earlier, on 29 October 1916, Jellicoe, then Commander-in-Chief of the Grand Fleet, had warned that 'our losses in merchant ships may, by the early summer of 1917, have such a serious effect on the import of food and other necessaries as to force us into accepting peace terms . . . .' Shipping losses from U-boats had reached a peak in April 1917, when 75 German submarines were operating. In that month total world shipping losses (most of which were due to submarines) amounted to 881,027 tons (545,282 of which were British). Jellicoe's warning had a great impact on the Government; but when he himself was put in charge of dealing with the submarine menace (as First Sea Lord), his performance disappointed Lloyd George. Though Jellicoe did set up the Anti-submarine Division of the Admiralty which took a series of measures aimed at destroying U-boats, he was resistant to the establishment of a convoy system. But the scale of shipping losses in April 1917 made it imperative that such defensive measures should also be taken. Hence in late April Lloyd George, who from mid-February had been slowly coming round to Hankey's view of the need for convoys, made it clear to the Admiralty that he would expect the convoy system to be given a trial. With Lloyd George at the door, the Admiralty reluctantly agreed to this (Hankey, 1961, pp. 645–51). The Admiralty may have been coming round to this decision, but Lloyd George certainly concentrated its mind and speeded up the implementation of the system, which proved a great success. As Trevor Wilson has observed of its trial, 'If there are such things as "decisive events" in this war, the first Gibraltar convoy must rank high among them' (Wilson, 1986, p. 436). Lloyd George went on to change the political leadership of the Navy, replacing Sir Edward Carson with Sir Eric Geddes as First Lord of the Admiralty in July 1917. At the end of the year he approved Geddes's action in sacking Jellicoe, who was replaced by Admiral Sir Rosslyn Wemyss (Grieves, 1989, pp. 48–54).

Lloyd George was also associated with a more interventionist food policy. From the outset of his premiership he had grasped that increased domestic food production would help to lessen the acute shortage of shipping space and help to husband Britain's diminishing financial resources. Thus he added a characteristic verbal flourish to a letter sent in his name to all British farmers: 'The farmers of this country can defeat the German submarine and when they do so, they destroy the last hope of the Prussian' (Davies, 1951, pp. 92–4).

In 1917 his Government carried out policies to increase food production which broadly had been advocated in 1915 by a committee chaired by Lord Milner, but then had been rejected because of ample international grain harvests and a still-adequate supply of shipping. Under the Corn Production Act of August 1917 farmers were encouraged by generous minimum prices to plough up land to grow wheat and oats but were threatened with the takeover of their land if they failed to make the best use of it. His government also maximized the quantity of cereals going into human food by allowing less of the grain that was ground to end up as animal feed and by blending some barley and maize with wheat flour. However, Lloyd George's government was slow to extend restrictions over the distribution of food, with limited rationing only introduced from late February 1918.

As the war dragged on, there were increased stresses on the home front as well as among combatants. The Government faced serious engineering strikes in May 1917 and further industrial unrest, until the German offensive of March 1918 led to renewed restraint on industrial relations for some months. Lloyd George attempted to respond to some of the root causes of this unrest by promising improved housing, a degree of worker-participation in industry (the Whitley Council scheme) and other measures of social reconstruction. Faced with peace overtures from Austria-Hungary and the publication by the Bolsheviks of Allied secret treaties (which showed that territorial gains and not just the restoration of 'Little Belgium' were among their war aims), on 5 January 1918 Lloyd George chose to make his own idealistic statement of war aims to a conference of trade union leaders in London. However, the much-feared social disintegration at home did not occur. Dissent was dampened down by the German offensive in March and then by the Allied advance from August 1918.

The speed with which the war ended caught politicians and administrators by surprise. In August 1918 few had expected the war to be over by that Christmas. This had unfortunate consequences for the planning of reconstruction (Cline, 1982). It also made urgent the making of vital political decisions.

The day after the Armistice Lloyd George called a General Election for December. He had for some months been considering holding one. With his usual political intuition he saw that the combination of his leadership with the Conservative Party would be hard to beat in the euphoria of the war's end, though earlier in the autumn he had still been toying with trying to work with Asquith and standing independently of other parties. However, such an option was secondary in his mind to continuing the coalition. In July 1918 the Whips had worked out a provisional allocation of seats between Coalition Liberals and Unionists. With the rapid end of the war Lloyd George threw in his lot with the Conservatives. As the General Election campaign progressed, Lloyd George's speeches swung away from Liberal ideas of a conciliatory peace and major social reconstruction at home to a harsher attitude of revenge. In this Lloyd George succumbed to the nationalistic popular mood of the moment.

He and Bonar Law sent out a letter of endorsement (dubbed 'coupons' by Asquith) to 374 Conservative, 159 Liberal and 18 National Democratic Party ('patriotic labour') candidates. Of these, 335 Conservatives, 124 Liberals and 10 NDP candidates were successful (with a further 48 Conservatives and 9 unendorsed government-supporting Liberals being elected). This gave Lloyd George's government the support of some 526 MPs against 181 others (73 of whom, being Sinn Fein candidates, did not take their seats at Westminster). Lloyd George's electoral triumph swept away Asquith and his most prominent supporters. In the new House of Commons there were 28 Independent Liberals, but 61 MPs taking the Labour Party whip.

There has been much effort spent by many historians in recent years to play down the differences between Lloyd George's wartime

92

government and those of Asquith. There is much truth in this. Of course there were many continuities between them. Wartime events and necessities did dictate policy; there was a process of learning in all spheres of government activity; and such matters were not confined to one government. But at the time among parliamentarians and others close to the heart of government, there was a widespread view that Lloyd George was single-mindedly committed to victory and that he brought dynamism of a special order to the premiership. By the end of the war the stress of responsibility had taken its toll on him, one sign being that his hair turned white. But he had the energy, the ability and the charisma to earn for himself the reputation of being one of Britain's great wartime leaders.

# 5

## *A Fit World and a Fit Land to Live in?*

Lloyd George reached the zenith of his career in 1919. He was the dominant figure in British domestic politics. Though not a party leader, he had won a massive victory in the December 1918 General Election. Indeed, at the time it was felt that the electorate had given him a personal endorsement. Moreover his international status was immense. He was a big figure among the Big Four (Clemenceau, Lloyd George, Orlando and Wilson) at the Paris Peace Conference. He redrew the map of Europe and, indeed, at that and at successive major conferences, remade the map of the world just as emperors, kings and aristocrats had done at the Congress of Vienna in 1815.

The use that Lloyd George made of the opportunities stemming from his apparently commanding political position after the Armistice of November 1918 has been the subject of considerable controversy. In 1961 A. J. P. Taylor was almost euphoric in his assessment.

> His balance sheet of success after the war was remarkable, perhaps more so than during the war itself. ... What he did after the war was all his own doing. Peace with Germany. Lloyd George alone, against Clemenceau and Wilson, secured a moderate territorial settlement, which did not deprive Germany of any 'ethnic' territory; he alone arranged reparations in such a way that they could be settled in agreement with Germany as soon as the Germans wanted to agree at all. Peace with Soviet Russia. Lloyd George secured this not only against his French allies, but against the majority of his own Cabinet including particularly Churchill. Peace with the trade unions. Lloyd

George circumvented the challenges from the railwaymen and the miners until they ceased to be dangerous. Peace with Ireland. Lloyd George performed the miracle which had defied every British statesman for over a century, or perhaps five centuries. . . . There was hardly a problem which he did not leave success behind him. The interwar years lived on his legacy, and exhausted it.

Though he went on to offset this by observing that these successes were undermined by the growing distrust of his methods: 'Men do not like being cheated even for the most admirable cause' (Taylor, 1961).

Kenneth O. Morgan, a major authority on all periods of Lloyd George's career, has written a largely sympathetic, though nevertheless critical, volume on his post-war Government in which he suggested that 'the Coalition, above all through Lloyd George himself, offered some kind of vision of social harmony and international conciliation which many young men and women entering politics in 1919 found neither ignoble nor undeserving of support' (Morgan, 1979, p. 375). Elsewhere Professor Morgan has given a verdict that 'Neither in its politics nor in its composition did the coalition of 1919–22 suppress its Liberalism' (Morgan, 1978, p. 41). However, other historians have placed more emphasis on the darker side of this Government's activities These have focused on such matters as Lloyd George's continued undermining of the Asquithian Liberals (Wilson, 1966), the savage nature of British policy in Ireland (Townshend, 1979), the alienation of much middle-class support (Cowling, 1971; Kinnear, 1973), the honours scandal (Searle, 1987), and Lloyd George's sometimes devious and sometimes very tough treatment of organized labour (Wrigley, 1990).

Peacemaking at Paris in 1919 is one of the more controversial policy areas of Lloyd George's post-war premiership. From an early stage even those involved in the negotiations on the victors' side felt that in a struggle between the high ideals of President Wilson's Fourteen Points and the French desire both for revenge and for security, the latter had won. Smuts and then John Maynard Keynes, in his influential *The Economic Consequences of the Peace*, concluded that the victors had imposed a 'Carthaginian Peace' on Germany. Keynes pointed out that the Armistice of November 1918 had been based on Wilson's ideals. But the Peace Conference, far from acting 'to discuss the details of their application' (as had been stated),

95

behaved in a very different manner, so much so that Keynes observed, 'The German commentators had little difficulty in showing that the draft Treaty constituted a breach of engagements and of international morality comparable with their own offence in the invasion of Belgium' (Keynes, 1919, pp. 51–60). Indeed, in the ensuing two decades there was a growing feeling among many British politicians and the electorate that Germany had been dealt with unfairly. In particular it was felt that the principle of self-determination had been applied selectively and generally to Germany's disadvantage; that the setting of unspecified and therefore unlimited reparations had been unreasonable; and making Germany accept the attribution of war guilt to herself and her allies had been unjust.

Lloyd George's own role revealed a blend of opportunism and idealism. But overall he showed an often keen determination to see that Britain was not left behind in gaining any spoils of war. Britain emerged from the peacemaking of 1919 and 1920 with substantial territorial gains, even if these were camouflaged as mandates rather than as direct annexations which would have affronted too blatantly President Wilson's sensibilities through breaching the principles set out in his Fourteen Points. The British Empire did achieve the old imperial dream of dominating an area from the Cape of Good Hope to Cairo, as well as one from Cairo through the Middle East to India, though its formal control of some of these Middle East areas was shortlived. Similarly Lloyd George was tenacious of British interests as a maritime power and he was eager to see that Britain got her share of reparations from Germany.

Yet there were sufficient residual Gladstonian principles within Lloyd George's outlook for him to warm to President Wilson's idealism whenever it did not restrain British gains or embarrass him politically with the Right in the House of Commons. However, these are important qualifications. Lloyd George needed no prompting from anybody to press for economically valuable territorial gains. During the Paris Peace Conference he spoke warmly of British gains of areas containing rich mineral deposits, observing in particular, 'I am told that Mesopotamia contains some of the richest oil fields in the world' (Wrigley, 1990, pp. 181–2). But on the matters of war guilt and reparations he did bend in the political wind that blew during the 'Khaki General Election' of December 1918.

During the election campaign Lloyd George played up to the nationalistic mood of the moment, making statements which undoubtedly he regretted within three or four months. Shortly before the Armistice he had been emphatic that 'a war indemnity had been ruled out, because beyond full reparation, Germany would have no means of paying further' (Lentin, 1984, pp. 12–13). Yet a month later, pursued by press and political critics of the Right, and faced with the financial implications of war debt and the funding of social reconstruction, Lloyd George allied himself with what he knew were unrealistic hopes of making Germany pay all the costs of the war (Kent, 1989, pp. 32–40). Similarly, to the alarm of many of his senior ministerial colleagues, Lloyd George endorsed the calls to put the Kaiser on trial. Here one can suspect that to Lloyd George's populism and opportunism was added a little of his old irreverence for royalty. Lloyd George gave a further hostage to fate in late November 1918 when he set up the special Cabinet Committee on Indemnity and included on it William Hughes, the aggressive and imperialistic Australian prime minister, Lloyd Sumner, a distinguished but belligerently anti-German judge, and Lord Cunliffe, the autocratic immediate-past-governor of the Bank of England. In appointing these men Lloyd George succeeded in upstaging much criticism from the Right in the ensuing General Election, but their adamantine refusal to compromise on the scale of reparations during the peace negotiations was severely to restrict Lloyd George's room for political manoeuvre (Lentin, 1984, pp. 19–21, 112–14).

Indeed, during the peacemaking held at Paris between January and June 1919 Lloyd George was most constrained when he was dealing with the issue of how much Germany would have to pay. He himself clearly expected that Germany would have to pay a substantial sum and that Britain would receive a large slice of it; but as to the actual amount, he was generally willing to accept however much satisfied his critics back in Britain. Colonel House, President Wilson's adviser, observed of Lloyd George when he was eager at one point to demand a large sum from Germany for immediate payment: 'He needed the sum purely to quiet his constituents; and he was quite willing to permit the Germans to default on it' (Lentin, 1984, p. 50). During the Peace Conference Lloyd George pursued various stratagems to get round the apparently irreconcilable facts that before the Armistice the Allies had specified only that 'compensation must be made by Germany for all damage caused to the civilian population of the Allies and their property by the aggression of Germany', whereas in the 1918 General Election he had joined the clamour to extract unlimited sums (not restricted to civilian damage) from Germany. Hence at the end of March 1919 he secured Jan Smuts's aid in

97

gaining President Wilson's assent to the dubious proposition that disabled soldiers' pensions could be encompassed in the category of 'civilian damage'. Similarly, Lloyd George was quick to support French proposals to postpone the fixing of the final sum of reparations until later, thereby avoiding a figure which his domestic critics would attack as too low and which President Wilson and Lloyd George's own common sense would deem too high for Germany to pay (Dockrill and Goold, 1981, pp. 49–56; Lentin, 1984, pp. 54–68). Putting off the evil day was a major trait of Lloyd George's ministerial career.

Lloyd George did make efforts to assuage French anxieties concerning France's security. In mid-March 1919 he offered France a military alliance as a guarantee against future unprovoked aggression by Germany, thereby getting Clemenceau to give up French insistence on detaching from Germany all German territory on the western side of the Rhine. This succeeded in removing a major impediment to the peace negotiations, as the British and Americans both took the view that 'the French schemes on this subject ... are short-sighted, selfish and quite impractical' (Dockrill and Goold, 1981, p. 35). However, there is a strong case for seeing what happened thereafter to this offer to France as a vintage example of Lloyd George's wiliness. In the ensuing weeks Lloyd George nibbled away at his promise – first excluding the British Empire from the guarantee, then reserving for Britain the assessment of what constituted 'unprovoked aggression', and finally making the British guarantee dependent on an American one being ratified (though, until the last, the American guarantee had been a separate and even a subsidiary matter). It is debatable whether he was characteristically back-pedalling after making a pledge which met the needs of the moment but the future implications of which he had not considered; or whether he was out to deceive Clemenceau from the start, as Antony Lentin suggests in his study of these negotiations (Lentin, 1991, pp. 124– 8). For all the shortcomings of Lloyd George's means to securing his ends at Paris, once Britain had achieved its main priorities Lloyd George did reassert the idealism that he had earlier expressed to the trade union gathering of 5 January 1918. In late March 1918 at Fontainebleau, he and his select personal advisers drew up a memorandum which included the aim that the peace treaty with Germany 'must be a settlement which will contain in itself no provocations for future wars, and which will constitute an alternative to Bolshevism, because it will commend itself to all reasonable opinion as a fair settlement of the European problem'. He also asserted:

I cannot conceive any greater cause of future war than that the Germany people ... should be surrounded by a number of small states, many of them consisting of people who had never previously set up a stable government for themselves, but each of them containing large masses of Germans clamouring for reunion with their native land.

As for reparations, he expressed the wise view 'that the duration for the payments of reparation ought to disappear if possible with the generation which made the war' (Lloyd George, 1938, pp. 405–16). In all this Lloyd George was putting pressure on the French to moderate their demands.

In restating liberal peace aims Lloyd George was also making a political point back home, namely that he was a major international statesman and the key figure in the coalition government and not just the puppet of the Conservative majority in the House of Commons. By securing what was in effect a resounding vote of confidence in the House of Commons on 16 April 1919, Lloyd George was proving to be more adroit than President Wilson in securing his domestic political position and making clear his authority to speak for his country throughout the rest of the peace negotiations. Perhaps he had learnt from the Maurice Debate of 1918 the benefits that followed from taking on his critics and exposing their parliamentary weakness (Wrigley, 1990, pp. 177–80).

For all this, Lloyd George was saddled with the need to appear to be tough with the Germans. When in May the harshness of the draft peace treaty as a whole was revealed, bringing a public reaction in Britain in favour of a settlement more in line with President Wilson's Fourteen Points, Lloyd George was swift to urge that liberal modifications should be made to the draft treaty on territorial matters. But it was notable that Lloyd George remained intransigent on the issues of reparations and war guilt, these matters being those most likely to cause him serious political trouble in the House of Commons. Lloyd George's last-minute rally to idealism left Clemenceau and Wilson cold. Antony Lentin has pointed to the irony of the situation in early June 1919:

Lloyd George, albeit out of pure expediency, was now embattled in defence of Wilsonism – while Wilson, in setting his face against concession, was objectively defending a settlement that bore all the marks of Lloyd Georgeism, a 'peace of shreds and patches', of compromises and 'deals', of those 'arrangements' which Wilson professed to, and indeed did, abominate. (Lentin, 1984, p. 99).

Overall, Lloyd George's performance at Paris should be seen as neither purely opportunist nor suffused with Liberal idealism. He was in part the Lloyd George who had pledged his political career to the cause of victory against Germany. He was also a political realist who knew that the British public expected Germany to suffer as a consequence of what was deemed to be her unbridled aggression. Yet while he expected Britain to receive substantial financial compensation from Germany, he was generally supportive of a moderate territorial settlement, deploring the creation of any new Alsace-Lorraine or the fostering of Bolshevism within the defeated nations (Elcock, 1972, pp. 212–14). But superimposed on all this were Lloyd George's characteristic political gymnastics, his jumping this way and then that to catch the prevailing political wind. Above all, he was encumbered by the pledges he had so rashly made in late 1918. As Lord Haldane noted at the time, 'Lloyd George always lives for the moment and never thinks of the lessons of the past' (Lentin, 1984, p. 27).

But what of his other memorable 1918 General Election pledges, those to do with making Britain 'a fit country for heroes to live in' (the actual wording he used in a speech at Wolverhampton on 23 November 1918)? Kenneth O. Morgan has commented:

the 1919 and 1920 [parliamentary] sessions were marked by a spate of social legislation without parallel since the heady days of the 1911 National Insurance Act. The Coalition became the vehicle for the New Liberalism *redivivus*. A range of new politics were put forward on a wide front, with the general acclaim of the political left, and reformers and welfare workers generally. (Morgan, 1979, p. 84)

The centrepiece of these reforms was Christopher Addison's housing programme. The Housing and Town Planning Act of July 1919 gave local authorities the duty to introduce housing schemes where they were needed, made provision for a subsidy from the Treasury towards the resulting housing loans and increased local town-planning powers. There were also extensions to the pre-war social welfare provisions: an increase in the rate of 10 shillings (50p) for the basic pension under the Old Age Pensions Act of December 1919; increased contributions and benefits under the National Health Insurance Act of May 1920; and, most important of all, the considerable extension of insurance coverage to those unemployed (now excluding primarily those in agriculture and domestic service) under the Unemployment Insurance Act of August 1920. Administratively the major innovation came with the establishment on 3 June 1919 of the Ministry of Health and the Scottish Board of Health, with the expectation that not only housing but poor-law changes would follow. The main educational measure had reached the statute book before the war ended: the Education Act of August 1918, which provided for the improvement of educational provision at many levels and included raising the school-leaving age to 14. But the Act's political architect, H. A. L. Fisher, who continued as President of the Board of Education in the post-war coalition, did build on that Act to encourage new school building, evening classes and day-continuation schools. In addition there was action on two of Lloyd George's old causes: the disestablishment of the Welsh Church was enacted in August 1919; as for the land, under the Land Settlement Facilities Act of the same month, powers were given to appropriate government departments to acquire land for smallholdings and to facilitate land settlement as well as for reclamation and drainage.

However, while there were numerous measures of social reform passed in 1919 and 1920, the two major ones proved to be flawed. The housing programme was affected by the continuation of wartime scarcities: notably of building materials and skilled labour. In addition, local authorities went to the money market for finance to fulfil their statutory duty to build houses while the post-war boom was on and when interest rates were moving up (from 6 November 1919). There was a provision in Addison's Housing and Town Planning Act which gave an open-ended Treasury subsidy to local authorities. After the use of the proceeds from a penny rate, the Treasury made up the difference between the capital cost of the house spread over a period of years and the income from rents set at a rate working people could afford. In these conditions this proved to be politically embarrassing as the cost escalated. Though a large number of houses were built under Addison's programme — some 170,000 — Addison himself was cast aside in March 1921 by Lloyd George, as the latter's own survival as Prime Minister increasingly depended on his appeasing Coalition Conservative backbenchers and much of the non-Labour voting electorate by cutting public expenditure (B. B. Gilbert, 1970, pp. 143−51; Morgan, 1979, pp. 90−8).

In the case of unemployment insurance the unduly optimistic premises on which its details were based were shown up in the acute economic recession from the end of 1920 into 1922 and by the prolonged high levels of unemployment thereafter. The 1920 Act worked on the assumption that unemployment would be lower than before 1914 and (not surprisingly) it did not anticipate structural unemployment, that there would be many people who would be continuously unemployed in the areas dependent on the old basic industries (coal, cotton, shipbuilding, iron and steel, wool) which were in permanent decline. It was also introduced too late. After five years of near full employment, contributions were collected from November 1920 as unemployment was rising; thus the lateness of the measure resulted in losing the opportunity to build up a large fund of money in good times (Gilbert, 1970, pp. 73–6).

Lloyd George's retreat from his promises to provide 'a fit country for heroes to live in' was most dramatically marked by his Government's adoption of the 'Geddes axe'. After the initial post-war fears of a potentially revolutionary working class, the British middle classes became more concerned about inflation and what they deemed to be excessive wage rises and lavish expenditure on social reconstruction. While elsewhere in Europe the middle-class backlash often took on a darker aspect, in Britain it remained constitutional, taking the form of by-election revolts against coalition candidates. After three by-election victories by Anti-Waste candidates in the first half of 1921 (defeating Coalition Unionists candidates in seats which should have been very safe for Unionists) Lloyd George took alarm, dispensing with Addison and that August appointing Sir Eric Geddes to chair a Committee on National Expenditure made up of businessmen. Geddes and his team set to work with vigour to bring down levels of public expenditure, especially on social services and the armed forces, an approach which was very much in line with Treasury policy. The armed services managed to escape the worse of the cuts but the 'Geddes axe' struck hard at the social reconstruction programme and education in particular (Morgan, 1979, pp. 243–66; Grieves, 1989, pp. 100–6).

However, if the 'Geddes axe' of 1922 was the most dramatic sign of the Government renouncing its social reconstruction programme, it was not an aberration. For the policy of currency deflation embarked on in 1919 ran counter to greatly increased public expenditure on reconstruction. Lloyd George, albeit possibly unwittingly, undermined social reconstruction when in August 1919 he accepted that tackling inflation should be a very high priority of his Government. That month he approved various measures which would ensure higher interest rates within Britain. Later, on 15 December 1919, Austen

Chamberlain, the Chancellor of the Exchequer, formally announced the Government's commitment to accept the recommendations of the Cunliffe Committee on Currency and Foreign Exchanges after the War. These involved restrictions on the money supply and Britain returning to the gold standard at the pre-war parity. In fact, by then the Government had embarked on deflationary policies which would negate an expansionary social programme. For a while Lloyd George appeared to hope he could both support deflation and yet maintain a major housing programme.

Lloyd George's hopes of social reform were also constrained by the burden of war debt. Too much of the cost of the war had been covered by raising loans within Britain rather than by heavier taxation. Early in the 1919–20 financial year ministers were faced with an internal debt of £6142.1 million, carrying an average interest rate of 4.65 per cent (compared to 3.25 before the war). Paying the interest charges on this debt was to take 34, 31 and 36 per cent respectively of the revenue of the Budgets of 1920, 1921 and 1922. Though Lloyd George and many other leading politicians seriously considered introducing a special tax on wealth that had been created during the war to lighten this burden of debt, the Conservative majority in the House of Commons ensured that such notions did not get far. Nor did the Government succeed in getting Germany to pay off Britain's war debt. On 5 August 1919 Chamberlain told his colleagues that 'it was not extravagance which was our danger so much as that we were trying to carry into effect at one moment more schemes for the benefit of the country than we are able to afford.' The undermining of social reconstruction was well underway before the 'Geddes axe' fell (Wrigley, 1990, pp. 234–42).

Lloyd George's attitude to Labour was also much affected both by the nature of the parliamentary majority that emerged from the 1918 General Election and by the pressures to deflate the economy. In the brief period between the Armistice and the General Election Lloyd George had approved substantial concessions to the cotton unions and the railwaymen. Trade unionists continued to make substantial gains in terms of reduced hours of work and higher pay, especially during the first seven months of 1919. Employers, fearful of even revolutionary let alone serious industrial unrest and eager to convert industry back to peace-time production in order to take advantage of the post-war boom, were more ready to acquiesce in such gains than they would be later, when they were more anxious about the price competitiveness of their goods for export.

103

However, once Lloyd George had put the General Election behind him he took a tougher line with the unions, taking very seriously the threat of a concerted Triple Alliance strike (involving the miners, railwaymen and dockers). Lloyd George used his ability to cope with industrial and social unrest as one major justification for his continued position at the head of the coalition. He was decisive in dealing with the wave of industrial unrest of January–February 1919, including what amounted to city-wide general strikes in Belfast and Glasgow. Then, in late February, he succeeded in getting the miners to delay strike action, at least to a less-propitious time for them, by appointing a Royal Commission on the Coal Industry: the Sankey Commission. By the calculated ploy of granting the railwaymen a substantial wage increase in March 1919, Lloyd George divided them from the miners. His resourcefulness in dealing with the severe industrial unrest of 1919 and also that fo 1920 to 1921 much impressed his ministerial colleagues.

However, to many trade unionists his actions appeared to be marked by trickery and deception. The miners clearly felt that Lloyd George and Bonar Law were pledged to abide by the majority report of the Sankey Commission, but they were disabused by Lloyd George in the House of Commons on 18 August 1919. Thereafter the miners were bitter and distrustful of Government action. Industrial relations in the coal industry were notably bad in 1920 and 1921 (and through to the General Strike of 1926 and beyond). Lloyd George also alienated many moderate and right-wing trade unionists by later disregarding the views of the National Industrial Conference which he had summoned in February 1919 at the height of the labour unrest. Then he had made much of it, building it up as a parliament for industry in which trade unionists and employers would consider industrial problems and to whose verdicts the government would respond with appropriate legislation. In fact, once the worst dangers of industrial unrest had passed, with the brief national railway strike of late September 1919, Lloyd George disregarded the National Industrial Conference (Wrigley, 1990, pp. 95–211).

He also alienated at different times both the Left and the Right in British politics with the policy swings on Ireland and on social reform. In the latter case, he alienated the Right when he persisted with major social expenditure after the heady days of the 1918 election; and then outraged the Left with the destruction of a sizeable part of the advances of 1918–20 by the severe public expenditure cuts of 1922. With Ireland the coercive policies of 1919–21 appalled the Left, while the Irish settlement of December 1921 incensed the Right.

By 1919 the old Home Rule policy was dying, if not dead. Lloyd George was not without blame. He had abetted the discrediting of John Redmond and the Irish Nationalist MPs in the negotiations of July 1916 that had followed the Easter Rising. Though it has been argued that the failure to secure a settlement then 'was not basically Lloyd George's fault at all' (Morgan, 1989, p. 91), there is, nevertheless, a case for deeming that he 'let the Nationalist leaders down very badly' by not backing that proposed settlement with his full political weight, even with the threat of resignation (Grigg, 1985, pp. 352−4). Similarly, in March 1918 his acceptance of the need to apply conscription to Ireland in order to gain much-needed additional manpower for the Western Front further boosted Sinn Fein's position against the Irish Parliamentary Party; though it can be added that it did much to help move many Unionist ministers from their hitherto intransigent stances to reluctantly accept the case for some measure of Home Rule in spite of the continued vehement opposition in Ulster (Ward, 1974). Yet, of course, Lloyd George's actions only added to the social and political changes which were undermining the position of the Redmondites and providing the background to the great victory of Sinn Fein in Ireland in the 1918 General Election.

Though Lloyd George was proclaiming himself to be 'still a Gladstonian Home Ruler' in October 1920 (Lawlor, 1983, p. 15), he was much less sympathetic to Irish aspirations after the war. This was in part due to the war having made him much more imperially minded. It was also due to his determination − as with social and industrial unrest − to display his capacity to stamp out disorder and to provide firm leadership.

In early 1919 Ireland was not only a difficulty for the British government in terms of law and order, it was also an acute embarrassment for the British delegation at the Paris Peace Conference. American and Dominion representatives were not slow to point to the contrast between British policy there and the principles of self-determination being aired at the Conference and applied to parts of continental Europe.

In this period Lloyd George and the government pursued a policy of half-hearted coercion, rather than implementing Home Rule immediately or, alternatively, responding to disorder with full-blooded coercion. From May 1919 Irish Volunteer action took more Royal Irish Constabulary lives. Such violence plus the conclusion of the Paris Peace Conference ended Lloyd George's resistance to pro-

105

claiming as illegal organizations Sinn Fein and the Dáil Eireann (which had been set up in January 1919 by the Sinn Fein MPs, all 73 of whom refused to take their Westminster seats). Sinn Fein was proscribed for various counties from July and then for all Ireland, while the Dáil was similarly condemned in September 1919. Lloyd George himself took an increasingly belligerent attitude towards the Irish situation. According to one account, he claimed in July 1919 that he could 'easily govern Ireland with the sword' (Townshend, 1975, pp. 13–31; Lawlor, 1983, pp. 38–44).

While Lloyd George and his Government were faced with growing violence in southern Ireland, from October 1919 their minds were further concentrated on the need to find a settlement by the prospect that the 1914 Home Rule legislation would come into effect when the last of the peace treaties was ratified. The realities of the Unionist predominance in Lloyd George's Government as well as the strength of Unionism in the northern Irish counties ensured that the Government recast the 1914 legislation. On 22 December 1919 Lloyd George stated in the House of Commons that the Government proposed to set up two Home Rule parliaments, one for the north as well as one in the south. As for the area to be covered by the one for Ulster, the matter was initially left open. But by February 1920 the Government had come down firmly in favour of the Unionists' desire to exclude the three predominantly Catholic Ulster counties yet include the two (Fermanagh and Tyrone) which had small Catholic majorities, thereby ensuring that they would be dominated by the large Protestant majorities in the other four counties. In his remarks in the Commons in December Lloyd George admitted that no scheme of Home Rule then could satisfy the nationalism of the south (Boyce, 1971, pp. 146–8; Lawlor, 1983, pp. 46–51).

Lloyd George thereafter took a very hard line against the rising tide of violence. From the end of 1919 recruitment took place among ex-servicemen in Britain for men to train with the Royal Irish Constabulary. These auxiliaries – or 'Black and Tans' – became notorious as paramilitary forces carrying out illegal and bloody re-praisals in nationalist areas. By his cold-blooded condoning of such actions, Lloyd George damned his liberal reputation with C. P. Scott and many others who had staunchly supported him. Indeed, with his statement 'We have murder by the throat' of 9 November 1920, he appeared to be proud of these activities. Labour leaders, such as Arthur Henderson, who had been life-long Home Rulers came to feel from early in 1920 that much more than Home Rule needed to be offered to nationalist Ireland. With the Black and Tan violence, Labour led a moral crusade against Lloyd George's government. On 9 December 1920 Henderson declared:

> By their actions the government's agents had produced in the minds of the Irish people the same effect as a mad dog loose in the public streets would produce. . . . They had made the forces of the Crown, which existed only to maintain law and order, the instrument of a blind and ruthless vengeance. This was not 'resolute government' but primitive barbarism. (*The Times*, 10 December 1920)

There was also growing disquiet among Lloyd George's ministerial colleagues.

The key to Lloyd George's stern attitude to Ireland appears to have been his belief that the Irish to wish to break away from the Empire was illiberal. As George Boyce has argued, he wanted to do business with an Irish leader who would 'stand up for the Empire as General Botha stood up for the Empire in South Africa'. He convinced himself that the old Liberal attachment to Home Rule was to do with strengthening both the United Kingdom and the Empire, not with disintegrating them. In dealing firmly with violent dissidents from such unity, he saw himself as something of a modern Abraham Lincoln (Boyce, 1971, pp. 150–3).

Yet often behind Lloyd George's attitude in 1920 and 1921 there was an awareness that in time he would have to negotiate a settlement, and he intended to do this from a position of strength. Thus on 13 October 1920 in a Cabinet discussion, he made it clear that he was not offering the nationalists something for nothing, and averred: 'Sinn Fein would have to come forward and bargain' (Boyce, 1971, p. 154). Lloyd George himself was ready to bargain, but in the first part of 1921 he was in no hurry to do so. However, from the time of the May 1921 elections to the southern Irish parliament he felt that perhaps Ireland was 'ripe for conciliation'. In those elections Sinn Fein candidates had been returned unopposed in 124 of the 128 seats (the other four being for Trinity College, Dublin, and were won by Unionists). Subsequently Lloyd George, having demonstrated to himself and to his political supporters the limits of effectiveness of bloody coercion, now convinced his ministerial colleagues that it was 'time for a gesture'. He may also have felt the need for a major policy achievement, given his Government's lack of success with unemployment or in resolving European problems and the severe cut-backs in social policy (Morgan, 1989, pp. 95—6). He built on the advocacy of both Smuts and King George V for a settlement, and invited Eamon de Valera (for the south and Sinn Fein) and Sir James Craig (for the north as the Ulster premier) to a conference in London. With the British Government agreeing to a truce (lifting a curfew, stopping all raids and searches, and limiting military action), the Irish Republican Army (IRA) also suspended all 'active operations' on 11 July 1921. From then until the London Conference began on 11 October there was a prolonged period of negotiating about the conditions for formal negotiations to begin.

Lloyd George's attitude on Ireland during the latter half of 1921 was that everything was negotiable within the parameters of Ireland remaining loyal to the Crown and staying within the Empire. He bluntly observed to his Cabinet colleagues on 7 September that 'men will die for ... throne and ... empire' but 'I do not know who will die for Tyrone and Fermanagh.' However, from the start to the end of the negotiations he made it clear that if Sinn Fein did not agree to a settlement within these limits, blood would again be shed. British troops returning from the Middle East and elsewhere would be available to be sent as a major force to Ireland (Lawlor, 1983, pp. 100—8).

Lloyd George moved with great skill to carry the Conservative Party with him. When back-bench diehards in the House of Commons moved a motion deploring the Government for 'entering its negotiations with delegates from Southern Ireland who have taken an oath of allegiance to an Irish republic and have repudiated the authority of the Crown', Lloyd George made it an issue of confidence and it was overwhelmingly defeated. Austen Chamberlain, the Conservative Leader, Birkenhead and Derby all backed him in seeking a settlement, provided that it safeguarded the wishes of the Ulster Protestants. They and other Conservative leaders successfully pressed the Conservative and Unionist annual conference held in Liverpool in mid-November to support Lloyd George's continuing efforts to achieve such a settlement.

Lloyd George then proceeded to negotiate in characteristic mesmeric manner. He was particularly successful at being imprecise on whether Ireland would be permanently divided. As George Boyce has commented, 'In 1916 he had attempted to gloss over the issue by postponing a final decision until after the war; in 1921 the device he adopted was "a boundary commission"' (Boyce, 1971, pp. 160—2). Lloyd George also exercised his intuition as to the strengths and

108

weaknesses of the personalities in the Sinn Fein delegation to help him divide them or to bring some towards a compromise. As usual, behind his coaxing and his charm he intimated his readiness to use the considerable resources of physical force at his disposal. With his uncanny sense of timing in negotiations, Lloyd George brought the proceedings to a successful climax on 5 December 1921, with the Irish delegation giving up their demand for a republic. Churchill later wrote:

> In the end, after two months of futility and rigmarole, scarred by outrages in Ireland in breach of the truce, unutterably wearied Ministers faced the Irish Delegates, themselves in actual desperation and knowing well that death stood at their elbows ... the Prime Minister stated bluntly that we could concede no more and debate no further. They must settle now; they must sign the agreement for a treaty in the form to which after all these weeks it had attained, or else quit; and further, that both sides would be free to resume whatever warfare they could wage against each other. This was an ultimatum delivered, not through diplomatic channels, but face to face ...    (Churchill, 1929, p. 305)

Thus Lloyd George secured a settlement; and in Dublin those who were prepared to accept the treaty (Arthur Griffith, the founder of Sinn Fein and his supporters) were left to fight it out with those who did not (Eamon de Valera, president of Dail Eireann, 1917–22, and his supporters). Lloyd George thereafter lost interest in the ensuing turmoil in Ireland. British troops were withdrawn and the issue of Ireland, at the forefront of British politics for most of the previous 37 years, receded for some 45 years. Yet, as with so many of Lloyd George's negotiating triumphs, it left a legacy of distrust. Many felt that they had been bamboozled by him. Churchill later commented:

> The event was fatal to the Prime Minister. Within a year he had been driven from power. Many other causes ... contributed to his fall; but the Irish Treaty and its circumstances were unforgivable by the most tenacious elements in the Conservative Party.    (Churchill, 1929, p. 307)

If during his post-war government Lloyd George 'solved' the Irish problem for several decades, he did so at considerable cost to his political position both with those on the Left and those on the Right of British politics.

109

Lloyd George's political standing was also eroded by other aspects of imperial and foreign policy. In India the immediate post-First World War years witnessed the greatest discontent between the Indian Mutiny (1857) and 1942. For the Right, the remedy was firm government. But the Secretary of State for India from July 1917 to March 1922 was the senior Liberal Coalitionist Edwin Montagu, who pursued a policy of moderate reform. In August 1917 Montagu had made a famous declaration in the House of Commons of the Government's intention to promote 'the increasing association of Indians in every branch of the administration, and the gradual development of self-governing institutions with a view to the progressive realisation of responsible government in India as an integral part of the British Empire'. Thereafter, with the Montagu—Chelmsford Report of 1918 (Chelmsford being the Viceroy, 1916—21) the Government had moved cautiously forward. Montagu also insisted that India should have a role at the Paris Peace Conference of 1919 with separate representation and being permitted to differ a little from the British representatives on policy. However, such progress was far too slow for Indian nationalism, both Hindu and Moslem; and yet it angered the Tory Right in Britain.

The situation deteriorated with the Amritsar massacre of 13 April 1919. Then, following serious unrest in that city which cost the lives of four Europeans, General Dyer had broken up a prohibited meeting by opening fire on an unarmed crowd, killing some 379 persons. Among many Britons living in India and among the Tory Right in Britain, Dyer became a hero and, after he had been forced to resign from the army, he became the recipient of a large public subscription. When a report on the Amritsar massacre was debated in the Commons in July 1920, 122 Conservative MPs voted against the Government while 93 supported it. Not surprisingly, the considerable show of support for Dyer did immense damage to Britain in Indian opinion. It also underlined the ominous divide between parts of the two wings of the coalition. Montagu remained as Secretary of State for India, still pursuing Liberal policies, until March 1922 when he resigned over Government policy towards Turkey (which had an adverse effect on Moslem opinion in India).

Lloyd George's attitudes to resurgent nationalism — be it Irish, Indian or Egyptian — in these years was far from sympathetic. He displayed a paternalism towards these peoples that was not very different from the attitudes of the great pronconsuls. Thus in October 1920, in the midst of the policy debates over the powers to be ceded

110

to a Dublin parliament Lloyd George gave the view: 'Irish temper is an uncertainty and dangerous forces like armies and navies are better under the control of the Imperial Parliament' (Townshend, 1975, pp. 36–7). In such matters he was not among the more radical of the Liberal Coalition ministers of his own Government.

With Russia, as with Ireland, Lloyd George alienated both Left and Right in British politics. Allied intervention on the side of the Whites in Russia came to be vehemently opposed by a very broad cross-section of the British labour movement. Later, after the White armies of Denikin and Kolchak had been defeated, even such unlikely figures as J. H. Thomas, Ernest Bevin and Arthur Henderson became sympathetic to direct action by trade unionists to stop the Government giving aid to the Poles against Soviet Russia. Soon a myth grew up that Labour in mid-1920 had forced Lloyd George to back down. Thus, a year later, Henderson proclaimed. 'There is no doubt whatever that the action of the Labour Movement early in August prevented open war with Russia' (Wrigley, 1990, pp. 267–72). In reality, even before Labour's Council of Action had been set up, Lloyd George had decided that public opinion would not support any fresh military action and had told the French premier this.

Yet the scale of Lloyd George's earlier support for Allied intervention in Russia had angered Churchill and also many of the Tory Right. They felt that if the Whites were given major support, then Bolshevism could be exterminated. Lloyd George clearly was not willing to commit himself and his Government to an all-out anti-Bolshevik crusade. He was well, aware of the war-weariness in Britain. In February 1919 he remonstrated with Churchill, advising him in a telegram: 'An expensive war of aggression against Russia is a way to strengthen Bolshevism in Russia and create it at home. We cannot afford the burden.' And yet there was an ambivalence in his attitude. He was not averse to extirpating Bolshevism on the cheap, if that proved possible. As A. J. P. Taylor has commented, 'Lloyd George was against intervention when it was not succeeding but he had bouts of enthusiasm for it whenever things were going well' (*Observer*, 1 November 1970). In this Lloyd George was probably in accord with his Conservative ministerial colleagues.

His desire to restore trade links with Russia also enraged many on the Tory Right. Lloyd George saw trade as the means by which Soviet Russia might be brought back into normal international relations and, indeed, might be tamed by the capitalist West. Moreover, as from 1920 it became very apparent that the British economy was

111

suffering from a massive drop in exports of her basic industrial goods, resuming trade with Russia seemed to be a significant way of helping the recovery of Britain's export industries and alleviating growing unemployment. However, to the Right, trade with Soviet Russia was – as Churchill graphically put it – to grasp 'the hairy paw of the baboon' (Morgan, 1979, pp. 135–8). The near-hysterical attitude of the Right to Bolshevism and Bolsheviks in this period is well encapsulated in the Bulldog Drummond yarns of 'Sapper' and the various adventure tales by John Buchan of these years. In spite of the anguish of those who had had assets expropriated in revolutionary Russia and of those dedicated to exterminating Bolshevism, Lloyd George did facilitate the visit to Britain of a Soviet trade delegation under Leonid Krassin in May 1920 and supported further negotiations which eventually led to the Anglo-Russian trade agreement of 16 March 1921.

Lloyd George also attempted to lessen Germany's diplomatic isolation. Between 1920 and 1922 he attempted to remedy some of Germany's major grievances stemming from the European peace settlement. Lloyd George himself took the lead in foreign policy, proceeding by means of what later came to be known as summit conferences. By early 1920 considerable doubts were being expressed in the House of Commons, largely on the Opposition benches, as to the practicality of the level of reparations expected of Germany – a debate prompted in large part by Keynes's *The Economic Consequences of the Peace* (1919). Lloyd George, at a series of conferences beginning at San Remo (April 1920), worked to moderate French actions towards Germany and in particular to prevent a French occupation of the Ruhr. While generally he did work to lessen the scale of reparations expected from Germany, nevertheless, as usual his attitude fluctuated according to short-term political needs. Given American determination to secure the repayment of her loans to Britain, Lloyd George was wary of advocating the drastic reduction of the amount due to Britain from Germany. Yet in May 1921 he was instrumental in getting all parties to agree to a programme of reparation payment, the London Schedule of Payments, which was more realistic than previous demands. But overall, like all other politicians of the victorious nations, he did not wish or dare to break with the political myth that Germany somehow could pay for all other countries' post-war reconstruction, any more than he would renounce a sizeable portion of Britain's share of reparations (Kent, 1989, pp. 92–6, 124–9, 141–2).

Lloyd George also supported territorial adjustments in Germany's

112

favour where he felt they were fully justified. Before the Treaty of Versailles was signed, the British Empire Delegation had been concerned at the proposed incorporation of Upper Silesia into Poland. Lloyd George had then secured agreement that a plebiscite should be held in that area within six to eighteen months of the Treaty being signed. Voting there in 1920 revealed some 60 per cent of the population in favour of being included in Germany. Lloyd George then successfully overcame French obstruction and passed the issue to the League of Nations, which in 1922 partitioned the area.

Again, Lloyd George's policies concerning France and Germany angered a small body of vehemently anti-German Tory backbenchers. These policies were also condemned by the Right-wing press which shared their views, notably the *Morning Post* and the *Daily Mail*. But those who took grave exception to his foreign policy in 1919–21 remained too few to challenge Lloyd George's grasp of the premiership.

Yet the surprise of the years 1919–22 was not that Lloyd George was ousted in October 1922 but, rather, that he stayed so long at the top of the greasy pole. By 1920, at least in southern England, there was growing discontent with the coalition among Conservative constituency activists. Even earlier, in mid-1919, well before the Anti-Waste by-election victories, there are signs that many middle-class voters were becoming more worried by inflation and high public expenditure than by the possibilities of Red revolution in Britain. As for Parliament, the dangers of Lloyd George's position were well illustrated early in the 1919 session when Sir Eric Geddes's Bill for a new Ministry of Ways and Communications was drastically altered and reduced in scope by Tories who were eager to repel state intervention in industry. So, in fact, Lloyd George's position rested on politically dangerous foundations from the time of the Conservative's success in the 1918 General Election. The fragility of this position became increasingly evident after he returned from his role as peacemaker at Paris and as the threat of Labour lessened.

However, it took accumulating distrust of Lloyd George and his ways, combined with a series of contentious government actions or policy failures in 1921 and 1922, to topple him. Michael Kinnear in a detailed study of the fall of Lloyd George has argued that most Conservative non-diehard MPs who rebelled against the coalition did so 'because of personal antipathy to Austen Chamberlain and Lloyd George rather than because of government policies' (Kinnear, 1973, p. 87). Lloyd George's position was undoubtedly weakened by the

113

resignation on grounds of ill-health of Bonar Law from the government and from the leadership of the Conservative Party in mid-March 1921. To most Conservative MPs Bonar Law had made up for the qualities that Lloyd George lacked. Chamberlain appeared too eager to proclaim coalitionism and to be too much a cipher of Lloyd George. Moreover, while Chamberlain himself still feared Labour, many Conservative MPs were aware that with the end of the post-war boom, trade unionism was on the defensive and employers were eager to roll back many of the gains ceded during 1915−20. Lloyd George's usefulness as a bulwark against 'Reds' had diminished.

Lloyd George's fall had much to do with a widespread distrust of, even a revulsion from, his methods. He appeared to be 'too clever by half'. Soon men such as Stanley Baldwin for the Conservatives and Arthur Henderson for Labour would make much of solid, worthy characteristics which were the antithesis of those so associated with Lloyd George as Winston Churchill and F. E. Smith (Lord Birkenhead). Lloyd George's enemies made the most of distaste for Lloyd George's ways when in the summer of 1922 they attacked him over the sale of honours. This was an issue which had been raised on earlier occasions by the Right, most notably by Sir Henry Page Croft in May 1919.

The Honours Scandal of the summer of 1922 was very much an indicator of the growing strain within the Conservative Party that arose from its continuing support for Lloyd George and the coalition. It was also itself important in undermining the Government. Those Tories who vehemently attacked Lloyd George and the Liberal Coalition Whips over selling honours were skating on thin ice. For Lloyd George was only doing what Conservatives had regularly done before − albeit in his case in a greater and more blatant way. Indeed, Lloyd George was very well aware that the Conservative Party was fully implicated in such activities. One of the more dubious recipients of an honour, William Vestey, was a Conservative nominee; one of the people touting honours at this time publicly implied that he worked for both wings of the coalition. But if Lloyd George expected the Tory hierarchy in the short run to protect him through protecting themselves, he was to find nevertheless that there was sufficient back-bench disquiet to give him a difficult time. The affair highlighted the general low estimate of his integrity among politicians and political commentators at the national level (Searle, 1987, pp. 350−76).

The strains within the coalition's supporters were not only about the premier's style. As well as the reaction against high public expenditure, accentuated by the severity of the 1920–22 economic recession, many Conservative back-benchers were also unhappy about a range of matters, from the Irish settlement of December 1921 to Lloyd George's seemingly perpetual summit diplomacy with its apparent often scant regard for the Foreign Office and his Foreign Secretary, Lord Curzon. Lloyd George's attempts to resolve the reparations issue, to bring both Russia and Germany back into normal relations with the rest of Europe, to help European economic recovery and to reassure the French faltered at the Cannes Conference of January 1922 and failed at the Genoa conference of April 1922. Whatever might have been achieved was dramatically undermined by the two 'pariah nations', Russia and Germany, making their own agreement at Rapallo on 16 April 1922.

Too many expectations had been raised before Genoa. French obduracy over Germany, the *impasse* in negotiations with Soviet Russia, the failure to achieve any substantial agreement on European peace and disarmament added up to failure at 'summit level' which was damaging to Lloyd George's prestige at home. Matters were made worse by savage attacks on the premier by *The Times* and other Tory newspapers. As Kenneth O. Morgan has commented, 'Right-wing critics, anxious not to have their country as policemen of the world, did not want her as the world's referee either' (Morgan, 1979, pp. 302–16; see also Fink, 1984; Orde, 1990, pp. 195–207). For them the final straw was Lloyd George's support for the Greeks against the Turks in Asia Minor, which resulted in British forces at Chanak facing Turkish troops fresh from their victory over the Greeks. Though a peaceful settlement was reached on 11 October 1922, Lloyd George had brought Britain close to a new war and – apart from New Zealand and Newfoundland – without support from others. Chanak, following on the failure at Genoa, did great damage to Lloyd George's standing in both his own Cabinet and in Parliament (Morgan, 1979, pp. 318–29).

However, until his fall Lloyd George remained a political Colossus in the country. Indeed Kenneth O. Morgan has offered the opinion that 'he retained wide public support to the end. One surmises that had Gallup Polls existed in those years a majority of the public would have continued to declare their confidence in their prime minister, at least until September 1922' (Morgan, 1974, p. 155). Whether this is so or not, Lloyd George's fall – like that of Margaret Thatcher in 1990 – was brought about by a revolt of those who had hitherto given him parliamentary support. At the Carlton Club on 19 October

115

1922, 187 Conservative MPs voted for independence for their party and thus for an end to the coalition.

Lloyd George's efforts in 1920 and 1921 to create a Centre Party around himself had failed. With the collapse of the coalition he was left with the Liberal Coalition MPs and a huge political fund he had amassed during his premiership. But the recently mighty Liberal Party was divided and weakened. He might be a foremost international statesman, but after 1922 within the British parliamentary system he was a lame duck — an impressive leader lacking sufficient parliamentary support.

# 6

## Lloyd George and the Liberal Party

Lloyd George left 10 Downing Street on 23 October 1922, never to return there as prime minister nor to hold public office of any kind. Although he was a politician with a massive international reputation, for the remainder of his career he was notable at home as a man who aroused hostility as bitter among a large section of his own party as among his severest critics in rival parties. The personal acrimony rampant among the top echelons of the Liberal Party undermined the party's standing with the electorate and blighted any possibilities of a major Liberal revival based on the new policies that Lloyd George sponsored.

Asquith's hostility to Lloyd George was in part about political style, as well as showing distaste for his post-war government's illiberal policies in Ireland and elsewhere and bitterness at his efforts to destroy the Independent Liberals as an electoral force. The building up of the role of premier into one more like that of leader (backed by a personal secretariat as well as the reorganized Cabinet); the marginalizing of the Foreign Office; the courting of the Press Lords; the honours bestowed in return for money on the rich but often socially dubious; the chicanery of Lloyd George's negotiating methods: all these were seen as aspects of a style which fell short of the best traits of British government in the Victorian and Edwardian periods. As John Campbell has observed, 'His rivals regarded him in rather the same way that amateur cricketers used to regard their professional colleagues. In the sporting sense, as in the social, Lloyd George was not a gentleman' (Campbell, 1977, p. 6). Lloyd George was very much a professional politician, with politics as an all-consuming passion. He gave little time to being lionized by polite society.

As well as dislike of his political style, doubts were frequently expressed as to Lloyd George's commitment to Liberal ideals and to the Liberal Party. A. J. P. Taylor on one occasion observed, 'For the Liberals he proved to be the cuckoo in the nest' (*Observer*, 24 July 1966). In this verdict he was referring to the post-1914 years. Indeed, for most of the period before 1914 it would be a view hard to sustain, when Lloyd George was repeatedly the regenerator of the Liberal Party as it drifted into the political doldrums. His eagerness to fan the embers of political life into flames by taking up contentious political issues was a recurring feature of his career before the First World War.

Unlike some of his Cabinet colleagues, he was a politician who had come up through grass-roots politics and in the pre-1914 period was very much mindful of the concerns of the party activists. In opposition he pushed the issues that nonconformist, temperance and land press-ure-groups loved most. In the mid-1890s he took pains to proclaim his commitment to the broad party programme (and so, by implication, criticized the way that the party leadership had allowed attention to Home Rule to exclude many of the other causes held dear by their supporters). Thus in December 1896 he declared at a large Liberal gathering in his constituency:

> There has been a good deal said in derogation of the Newcastle Programme [1891] but no genuine Liberal would wish to with-draw one item of it from the Liberal policy. There are many Liberals who would wish to add to it. (*North Wales Observer*, 18 December 1896)

But once in office, as Professor Hamer has observed, his attitude was somewhat like that of Joseph Chamberlain who 'sought to solve several of the "faddist questions" without any reference to the pressure groups themselves' (Hamer, 1977, p. 6). Lloyd George did con-sult many of the Liberal pressure-groups when Chancellor of the Exchequer, but his policies were usually far removed from their prescriptions.

Asquith, for one, usually admired Lloyd George's political energy during the Liberal Governments. He appreciated Lloyd George's efforts to revive the fortunes of the Government both after the Lords had vetoed the Bills of particular appeal to nonconformists in 1906–8 and after the two General Elections of 1910. Lloyd George eschewed the fatalism that beset some of the Cabinet and Liberal backbenchers, who appeared willing to do nothing controversial while drifting towards

118

inevitable electoral defeat. Thus in 1912 Arthur Murray, the brother of the Master of Elibank, objected to the proposed land campaign, observing: 'the Liberal Party cannot be in power for ever, and this is a fact that should be recognised by some of the wild men on our side' (Emy, 1971, p. 50). Asquith's support for Lloyd George over the Poeple's Budget and other issues, such as national insurance and the land, was very important. Asquith not only appreciated Lloyd George's dynamism but also his usually uncanny sense of the popular mood. Indeed, Asquith sometimes tried out ideas on Lloyd George, saying to others that he was 'an excellent foolometer' (Brett and Esher, 1938, vol. 3, p. 61).

As for his commitment to Liberal ideals and issues, the record is indeed mixed, even before 1914. He supported Home Rule but often showed that he preferred Home Rule All Round as a policy. Nevertheless, he stiffened some of his Cabinet colleagues against backtracking on the issue after the second electoral verdict of 1910.

He supported Free Trade but he never made it a matter of pure faith which could not be defiled by exceptions. Some of his measures at the Board of Trade trespassed on the edges of Free Trade but most revealed common sense. Though in 1910 he dangled the possibility of some instalment of tariffs in his conversations with Unionist leaders when trying to interest them in negotiating a coalition government, in his written proposals he made only a mention of tariffs with no indication of a likely major policy change. Later, he was to allow significant incursions during his post-war coalition government, following on from the wartime breaches – the McKenna Duties – which had been introduced under Asquith. These were largely, but perhaps not entirely, due to political expediency. But overall he seems to have seen Free Trade as the best, but not a perfect, trade policy and treated it as a practical matter rather than as a matter of ideology. When in 1932 the National Government ended Britain's Free Trade Policy, Lloyd George did not hesitate to use this issue to embarrass former Asquithian colleagues who remained in the Government. Of Runciman he observed in the Commons:

> I have heard many of his speeches on the subject, and I have read some of them since and, when I used to read them or hear them, stating the pure doctrine, I felt my own shortcomings and I said, 'I cannot come up to that standard.' I look at him now just as one looks at the skeleton of a departed Free Trader, and I say, 'Alas, poor Yorick. We knew him well, and still do.' (268 *H. C. Deb. 5s*, c.1173; 12 July 1932)

While one can wonder about the extent of Lloyd George's commitment to various traditional issues, and even assess his ideological purity on them, the important fact remains that he played a key role in reviving not just the Liberal Governments but Liberalism itself in the pre-1914 period. After the severe disappointments on social issues of the 1892–5 Liberal Governments, there ensued a rethinking of the nature and priorities of Liberalism by numerous intellectuals on the edges of the party. Central to such reformulations was a recognition of the need for the state to take an active role, thereby putting a lesser emphasis on the importance of individual effort and independence than the older Radicalism had done. As Michael Freeden has observed, 'A perusal of Edwardian social legislation undisputedly reflects new liberal themes such as the ultimate moral responsibility of the state in conjunction with individual activity, the linkages among social problems, and the redistribution but not total elimination of private wealth' (Freeden, 1990, pp. 186 and generally 175–90). Lloyd George himself moved from his old Radical postures of the 1890s to being the most significant of the few Liberal ministers who actively brought in policies of a New Liberal kind.

In taking up new approaches to social problems and to public finance Lloyd George was acting as a pragmatic politician. He saw the need for social welfare measures and he took the best ideas available, adapting them as he felt desirable and politically necessary. With energy and political courage he planned and campaigned for the People's Budget, national insurance and land reform. In finance he produced two major innovatory Budgets (1909 and, for all its flaws, 1914) and used them as instruments of social policy, making in them a substantial shift in the burden from indirect to direct taxation. Above all, he showed the viability of Free Trade finance to underpin major social reform, so charting a middle way between the twin challenges of Unionist protectionism and Labour on the Left.

Lloyd George had a keen appreciation of how Socialists had displaced Liberal parties in several continental European countries. Following the success of Keir Hardie and John Burns as Labour candidates in the July 1892 General Election, Lloyd George had told a meeting of quarrymen in his constituency that if working men joined Liberal Associations and then ensured that parliamentary candidates reflected their views, 'The demand for a Labour Party will . . . be unnecessary.' By late 1904 he was warning that the Liberal Party would face the same fate of those in Germany and Belgium unless 'the Liberal Administration which we can see on the horizon' took action to meet 'the legitimate claims of labour' (Wrigley, 1976, pp. 24–6).

Lloyd George was very aware of the need for Liberals and Liberalism to move with the times. In 1913 he observed that they were then 'carving the last few columns out of the Gladstonian quarry'. Soon after becoming premier, he told C. P. Scott: 'Old hidebound Liberalism was played out; the Newcastle programme [of 1891] had been realized. The task now was to build up the country' (Wilson, 1970, p. 257). Lloyd George's ideological flexibility was not all opportunism. It served his party well before 1914.

Lloyd George, then, before 1914 was pre-eminently the Liberal politician who offered to the electorate a viable Free Trade and Liberal alternative to either tariff reform politics or to the mixture of trade union and social welfare issues plus a dash of socialism that was the main substance of the pre-1914 Labour Party campaigns. Before 1914 Labour was growing in strength: very much so in some areas of Britain. But it took the First World War with its transformation of politics and of the labour market to move Labour from being a junior element in a Progressive Alliance to being a political party widely expected to take power in a matter of time. The divisions at the top of the Liberal Party added to the benefits which the war-time economy bestowed on Labour.

Lloyd George, in giving priority to organizing for victory over all else in 1915 and 1916, alienated many of his former colleagues. Indeed, his impatience to secure conscription and a small war committee gravely harmed what hitherto had generally been a good relationship with Asquith. When he replaced Asquith as premier, relations plunged very low indeed, and his relations with Asquith's closest associates even lower. Yet with Asquith broadly supporting the government and the war effort, surely December 1916 did not mark an irreversible breach in the Liberal Party nor ensure its later decline? However, during 1917 and 1918 the lines between Asquith's and Lloyd George's Liberal followers continued to harden. While Asquith – Maurice Debate apart – avoided a major parliamentary split between the two groups of Liberals, he nevertheless declined offers in May 1917 and in November 1918 to join Lloyd George's Government. On the earlier occasion Asquith was still condemning a small war committee, commenting, 'self-respecting statesmen cd. not be expected to take part in such a crazy adventure'. As for Lloyd George, he observed, 'In my judgement he had incurable defects, both of intellect and character, wh. totally unfitted him to be at the

121

head' (Wilson, 1966, pp. 122–4). Had Asquith been able to swallow his pride and accept such an offer then, presumably, the Liberal Party's history, at least in the immediate post-war period, would have been transformed.

On Lloyd George's part, his decision to fight an immediate post-war election in harness with the Conservatives, thereby to continue the coalition in order to 'win the peace', was understandable but extremely damaging for the Liberal Party. While 133 Liberals who supported Lloyd George won their seats, only 28 of Asquith's followers were successful. Asquith and all his leading associates were defeated, an outcome which, naturally, greatly added to the personal bitterness they felt towards Lloyd George. Lloyd George himself gained all the power and prestige he could have hoped for; in the first half of 1919 he was at the zenith of his career. But his triumph was short lived, and he had grievously damaged the instrument (the Liberal Party) of his rise to the fore of public life.

While the 1918 General Election is rightly seen as a turning point in the fortunes of the Liberal Party, the period 1919–22 does not always get the equal billing that it deserves. For in these years Lloyd George used his power and his prestige to try to smash the Independent Liberals and to win over their voters to his coalition. This was part of his efforts to reconstruct around himself a new Centre Party, united in its opposition to socialism. From July 1919, soon after his return from peace-making in France, Lloyd George floated the notion of a new 'national' party which would build on the unity of purpose displayed during the war. This would be a broad church acceptable to all but reactionaries and Bolsheviks. However, when he tried to push forward the creation of such a party in March 1920 his own Coalition Liberal colleagues revolted at the proposal. The idea would have been even less well received among the Conservative Coalitionists. By early 1922 Lloyd George found that many Conservatives would not countenance a further General Election fought on coalition lines, let alone consider a new political grouping to suit Lloyd George.

Not only did Lloyd George wage electoral war on the Independent Liberals, but many of the coalition's policies were ill-received by Liberals. Such matters as intervention in Russia and the use of the Black and Tans in Ireland encouraged many former Liberal supporters to look to Labour. Indeed, during 1919–22 Labour, in spite of dull leadership, steadily established itself as the most likely future alternative to a Conservative government. In the 1922 General Election which followed Lloyd George's fall Labour won 142 seats to the Liberals'

116 (47 explicitly supporting Lloyd George, 41 Asquith and 28 prefixless) (Kinnear, 1973, p. 196).

In spite of the precarious position of the Liberals, now very clearly the third party in the House of Commons, it took Stanley Baldwin's declaration of the need for Protection and his calling of a General Election in October 1923 to reunite them around Free Trade. Before that Lloyd George had campaigned in the country almost as a born-again Liberal, while Asquith and his associates had made clear that Liberal Coalitionists could only return in the manner of very penitent prodigal sons.

The bitter hostility felt to Lloyd George, even with the Liberal reunion of 13 November 1923, is well illustrated by Sir John Simon's attitude. In late 1919 Simon had attempted to return to Parliament in a by-election in Spen Valley but had been opposed by a Liberal Coalition candidate. This had allowed Labour to win the seat. Three weeks after the reunion in 1923 Lloyd George sent Simon the general election message: 'Sincerely hope the electors of Spen Valley will have the advantage of securing your brilliant abilities for their services and the service of the principles of Liberalism in Parliament.' Simon simply filed this with his political papers, attaching to it a short memorandum stating: 'The consummation of Liberal Unity. Contrast with Lloyd George's telegram trying to defeat me in the by-election of 1919. I did not publish the annexed, for Liberal unity only disgusted some of my keenest supporters and would not gain me a single vote' (Simon Papers).

Yet while the reunion of the Liberal Party did not extinguish much of the personal bitterness in the party, Lloyd George soon won over some of his critics by his greater willingness to adapt to new ideas than Asquith and his close associates. He had little difficulty in portraying the Asquithians as worshippers at the shrine of a Liberalism that had become frozen in time. Lloyd George recognized that political and economic circumstances had been greatly changed by the massive upheaval of the war. Hence he viewed with impatience attempts to hark back only to the issues of 1914 or of even before 1908. Such an attitude was also politic, given his need to defend his record during 1919–22. But he himself did cling to several themes of his earlier career, notably the land and nonconformist concerns.

Lloyd George's willingness to take up new ideas and to sponsor the reformulation of Liberal policies won back the support of men such as Charles Masterman. Later Lucy Masterman recalled: "'I've fought him as hard as anyone," Masterman said to me, "but I have to confess, when Lloyd George came back to the party, ideas came back to the party." Their causes of difference began to retreat into the past' (Masterman, 1939, pp. 345–66). Even more striking was the support that he gained between 1926 and 1929 from Keynes, given both the latter's severe criticisms of his performance at the Paris Peace Conference made in *The Economic Consequences of the Peace* (perhaps rendered more severe by Keynes believing that Lloyd George, in 1919, was going to sack him) and his personal friendship with Asquith (Davenport, 1974, p. 45). Indeed, the bisexual Keynes even confided to his wife on one occasion in the late 1920s: 'I had a terrible flirtation with Ll. G. yesterday, and have been feeling ashamed of myself ever since!' (Hill and Keynes, 1990).

After the 1923 Protection versus Free Trade General Election, Lloyd George was a politician who needed a cause, for after that election his earlier hopes of creating a new centre-based coalition government were greatly reduced. His former secretary and foreign policy adviser Philip Kerr urged him to tackle the issue of how best to organize British industry. Lloyd George responded both by sponsoring an inquiry into Britain's fuel resources (published that July as *Coal and Power*) and with an article in the Liberal weekly the *Nation* in April 1924 in which he harked back to his old national development arguments. 'Let us overhaul our national equipment in all directions – men and material – so as to be ready, when the moment arrives, to meet any rival on equal or better terms in the markets of the world' (Campbell, 1975, pp. 96–8). His call for public investment in the infrastructure of the economy received a positive response from those Liberals who had been active at various conferences in recasting Liberal policies since 1920 and (from 1921) at the Liberal summer schools. By July 1926 the *Nation* was asking, 'Is it too much to hope that from the union of the gifts of Mr Lloyd George and the Summer School there may emerge the new radical impulse which we need?' (Freeden, 1986, p. 104).

Characteristically, Lloyd George's major policy initiative before Asquith departed from the leadership of the Liberal Party was an investigation into the land. These proposals, which had been in preparation for two years, were published in the autumn of 1925 as *The Land and the Nation* and *Towns and the Land*, known respectively as the Green Book and the Brown Book (from the colour of their covers). The first volume, on rural land, called for the state to resume possession of all economically viable land. In this, and in its proposal to help the good farmer but to evict the bad, Lloyd George was

124

looking back to the war-time controls established under the Corn Production Act of 1917. In promising to create employment by encouraging a return to the land, he was harking back to an old radical tradition and on a lesser scale to a measure passed by his own post-war government. These proposals, and especially that of state control of the land, provided the occasion – as had the People's Budget in 1909 – for an outflow to the Conservative Party of rich and influential Liberals such as Sir Alfred Mond. While many of the leading figures of the Liberal Summer School – such as Ramsay Muir and Ernest Simon – supported it, Keynes and others could work up no enthusiasm for concentrating on the land as a key issue and trying to re-run the pre-1914 land campaigns (Campbell, 1975, pp. 99–100).

Lloyd George's new land campaign, launched before a crowd of 25,000 at Killerton Park, Devon, on 17 September 1925, was a major attempt to thrust a Liberal Party issue to the centre of British politics. But like his pre-1914 initiatives, it also promoted Lloyd George. As with the 1909 Budget, Asquith was cautiously supportive but pressed on him the need to carry the party with him. In December 1925 Lloyd George agreed to dilute the original rural proposals; nationalization was dropped and varieties of tenure were on offer. With these major modifications both the rural and urban land policies were adopted as Liberal Party policy by a special Land Convention held in London in February 1926. John Campbell has given the reasonable verdict that this was Asquith's 'last successful exercise in Liberal leadership':

> Never allowing his acolytes to rush him into outright criticism, but always giving Lloyd George qualified encouragement, he succeeded in getting the Green book stripped of its 'most questionable features' without unpleasantness, modified in keeping with his own more moderate temper, and officially adopted as the still distinctive policy the party needed. (Campbell, 1977, p. 128)

Yet internecine bitterness remained rampant in the reunited Liberal Party. It fed on resentments over Lloyd George's actions during the war and his attacks on the Independent Liberals after the war. It was further fuelled by Asquithian distaste for Lloyd George's huge political fund, deemed to be ill-gotten lucre that degraded the highest standards of public life; yet their disdain was combined with near-fury that it was not freely available to benefit them. Moreover, there were certain jealousies aroused by Lloyd George's return to the role of Crown Prince to Asquith, most obviously aroused in Sir John Simon who had been expected to inherit the leadership when Asquith retired. But there were many in British political life, and not just Asquithians, who could join with Sir Alfred Mond in condemning Lloyd George as 'a leader who had lost all political conscience, except a burning desire somehow to climb back into office'. Indeed, during the 1920s Lloyd George moved this way and that for political advantage, sometimes veering towards Conservatives to explore possibilities of a new centre grouping and at other times making advances towards Labour. As Michael Bentley has concluded, 'Little that Lloyd George did between 1924 and 1927 can be reduced to conformity with a single system of thought' (Bentley, 1977, p. 98).

Relationships with Labour proved to be one area which revealed particularly damaging differences in the Liberal Party. Resentments within the party exploded during the General Strike of 1926. They re-emerged and resulted in further damaging splits during the second Labour government of 1929−31, though during the time of the first Labour government of 1924 bad feeling within the Liberal Party was not over policy differences.

With the hung Parliament that resulted from the December 1923 General Election both Asquith and Lloyd George were agreed that there was no realistic alternative to putting Labour into office, even though from an early stage Lloyd George recognized, as he told C. P. Scott on 2 February, that: 'If Labour succeeds, they get all the credit; if it fails, we get the blame for putting them in power' (Wilson, 1970, p. 455). Lloyd George had little optimism that Labour would achieve much. Moreover, from the First World War onwards he and MacDonald disliked each other intensely. A month after the formation of the first Labour Government he observed to Megan: 'Ramsay is just a fussy Baldwin − and no more' (Morgan, 1973, p. 202). At first he put on a great show of encouraging Labour to come forward with radical proposals, but later he concentrated on differences. In his rhetoric in Parliament and in particular in his vigorous defence of Liberal sensitivities, Lloyd George made clear his supreme fitness to be Liberal leader. But, as in 1915−16, he was probably asserting his position in the pecking order, underlining his position as Asquith's Crown Prince. He roused Liberal activists' fervour with speeches in which he deplored Labour's failure to work as in 1906−14 in a progressive alliance. In Wales, on 22 April 1924, he complained:

126

Liberals are to be the oxen to drag the Labour wain over the rough roads of Parliament for two or three years, goaded along, and at the end of the journey, when there is no further use for them, they are to be slaughtered. That is the Labour idea of co-operation. (Campbell, 1977, pp. 94–5)

Yet, though Lloyd George wound up his own National Liberal Party organization in March 1924, throughout the first Labour Government's life he was adamantine in his refusal to provide the Asquithian-dominated Liberal Party organization with funds. As a result only 343 Liberal candidates, not the hoped-for 425, stood in the 1924 General Election (though very late in the day Lloyd George did provide £50,000 – half the money that was expected of him). With 42 MPs elected, compared with the 158 elected in 1923, LLoyd George's name was mud among the Asquithians. But his reluctance to provide adequate funds for a General Election (which he hastened by undermining the Labour Government) was probably more a sign of Lloyd George's stubbornness and his determination to wrest at least partial control of the Liberal Party machine than some more long-sighted Machiavellian action to oust Asquith, to smash his own party and to rule the rump (as is suggested by John Campbell, 1977, p. 89).

The General Strike of 1926 provided the occasion for a final show-down between Lloyd George and Asquith. As in December 1916, Asquith, egged on by his supporters, chose the wrong ground on which to challenge Lloyd George. Asquith sympathized with Baldwin in seeing the General Strike primarily as a constitutional issue, or even as a matter of law and order. Lloyd George, while condemning the General Strike, also criticized the Government for permitting a trade dispute to escalate into a major crisis. Indeed, Lloyd George made these points in the letter he sent when absenting himself from the Liberal Shadow Cabinet meeting on 10 May. In it he went on to state, 'I prefer the Liberal policy of trusting to conciliation rather than force', and then endorsed the Archbishop of Canterbury's efforts to mediate. On 20 May Asquith, after consulting his associates, sent by special messenger a letter to Lloyd George in which he deplored 'the course you have pursued in the greatest domestic crisis which the country has had to confront in your time or mine'. This letter, which Lloyd George with humour dubbed 'an angry bull of excommunication', went on to state that Asquith felt that his refusal to attend the meeting on 10 May was 'impossible to reconcile with my conception of the obligations of political comrade-ship'. Lloyd George, advised by C. P. Scott and others, responded in a tone of sweet reason. He enquired 'if there is to be another schism in the party, one would like to know what it is about' (Sylvester, 1947, pp. 147–58). Asquith and his associates found to their cost that the bulk of Liberal Party members supported Lloyd George's approach to the General Strike and did not approve of the attempt to remove him from the Liberal leadership. In mid-October a bitter and defeated Asquith retired as leader of the Liberal Party.

With Asquith gone, Lloyd George was leader in fact but not in name. For the Asquithians ensured that the party in opposition went back to the old practice of having separate leaders in the Commons and the Lords. So Lloyd George remained, as he had since Asquith lost his seat in the Commons in the 1924 General Election, chairman of the Parliamentary Liberal Party in the House of Commons. He had spent his adult life aspiring to lead the Liberal Party, but now found that the long-sought-after fruits were sour. Even when Asquith's loyal supporters withdrew from major posts in the Liberal Party machine, they joined Grey to form a new body, the Liberal Council, which acted as a focus for opponents of Lloyd George within the Liberal Party (Wilson, 1966, pp. 339–41). After the 1929 General Election, Grey was still grumbling about Lloyd George. To Lord Gladstone on 3 August 1929 he wrote:

> even if Lloyd George parted with all his fund, the Liberal Council would not dissolve, as we had no confidence in Ll. G. as leader. This distrust of him was widespread and I felt it so strongly that I should probably take no part on Liberal platforms at the next election, if Ll. G. was leader.

He added of Lloyd George that 'he must be the most prominent person in any party he attached himself, but that he was a disintegrating force and fatal to Liberal success' (Gladstone Papers; British Library Add. Ms. 45, 992, f.159).

Lloyd George, of course, could give as good as he could take. Indeed, on 13 May 1926, just after Lloyd George had declined to attend the Shadow Liberal Cabinet, he had been sounding out Arthur Henderson about possible Liberal–Labour co-operation in the House of Commons. Henderson reported to Ramsay MacDonald that 'the only condition was that we should take up his land scheme in its original form and not as amended by Liberal Conferences' (Wrigley, 1991, p. 54). Clearly, Lloyd George had been hoping to use Labour as a counter in swinging Liberal policy back in a direction unpalatable to the Asquithians. Indeed, he had given a hint of his true views at the Liberal Land Convention of February 1926 when he declared:

> It would be fatal to wash out all the vitality of Liberalism. Agreement achieved in that way would be disastrous to Liberalism. It is no use taking the vitamins out of food, and therefore, while we must do our best to reach agreement, we must do so without sacrificing the vitality, the energy, the efficiency, the appeal and the inspiration of our policy. (Campbell, 1977, p. 127)

In such sentiments he was being consistent with his past, with the views he had expressed when applauding Joseph Chamberlain's early Radicalism when trying to stir up Liberal support in his own marginal seat in the 1890s and during the years 1908–14.

Lloyd George's last major chance to regenerate the Liberal Party was to be during the three years after Asquith's retirement. In 1926 he provided the leading figures of the Liberal Summer School with £10,000 to conduct a detailed inquiry into industrial policy, the need for which had frequently been suggested by Philip Kerr. During that October Kerr, when writing on industry, commented to Lloyd George, 'I am sure the Liberals have an immense opportunity in the next couple of years if they will really think out their economic policy' (Lothian Papers, GD40/17/223, f.232–33). The Liberal Industrial Inquiry was carried out by many of the liveliest Liberal minds of the time, including Keynes, Ramsay Muir, Walter Layton, E. D. Simon and Lloyd George himself. E. D. Simon later recalled of weekend meetings at Churt:

> He was a perfect host; he gave us the benefit of his vast experience; he never made the least attempt to use his position to influence our report, except by contributing to the discussion on an equality with all other members. (Hodgson, 1943, p. 183)

The findings of the Inquiry were published in February 1928 as *Britain's Industrial Future* (the Yellow Book).

The Yellow Book offered a middle way between socialism and *laissez-faire*. It declared: 'Liberalism stands for Liberty; but it is an error to think that a policy of liberty must always be negative, that the state can help liberty only by abstaining from action, that invariably men are freest when their government does least.' It boldly stated,

129

'The grievances of today are mainly economic', and it called for a mix of state and private action to deal with the industrial problems of Britain. In its details it built in some of the earlier, more interventionist Liberal policies. Thus in industrial relations it proposed minimum wages in industries (so building on earlier wages boards), layers of joint committees in industry (so building on the Whitley committees), and schemes for employees to hold shares and share profits in their firms. It also had a major section on Lloyd George's old theme of national development, which called for policies ranging from reviving agriculture to major public works, thereby absorbing unemployment. Among the proposals stemming from Keynes were a Board of National Investment to channel capital towards these major development projects, similar to that operated by the government of India, and (following Sir William Beveridge), 'as an essential instrument of better and wiser government the creation of ... an Economic General Staff'.

With fresh, new policies, the Liberals faced the electorate with greater confidence. The problem, however, was to get their message over. Kerr was percipient in his comments on the Yellow Book in a letter to Lloyd George on 7 February 1928:

> *Britain's Industrial Future* strikes me as extremely good. It is so good, in fact, that it is a poor electioneering document. It lacks the impact, from the political point of view, of a simple rallying cry like Protection or Nationalisation. (Lothian Papers, GD 40−17−229, ff.348−9)

Lloyd George, so often in tune with popular attitudes, simplified the Liberals' new message by highlighting in the three months before the 1929 General Election one major and highly topical thread of the Yellow Book: unemployment. So the pamphlet *We Can Conquer Unemployment* was produced, detailing Liberal schemes to create work for an additional 600,000 people. Lloyd George and his colleagues, of course, could not foresee that soon the political problem would be not just to cut away at a fairly static 1.1 million unemployed but to face a rapidly increasing number of people out of work. It reached some 2.5 million by the end of 1930.

Lloyd George's efforts contributed to a rise in the Liberal vote from the poor 2.9 million of the 1924 General Election to 5.3 million. But the number of seats only increased from 40 to 59. Lloyd George was left with the problem of exerting maximum Liberal influence on a minority Labour Government in a hung Parliament. From the outset his task was made harder by Asquithians newly returned to the Commons who made it clear to MacDonald that Lloyd George did not command a united party. Sir Donald Maclean, who worked with Grey on the Liberal Council, let the Labour Party leader know that they 'decline to be controlled by anyone connected with the L.G. group' and that they 'had determined that you should have a fair chance and they would do all that was possible to support you, particularly if they could have sometimes in advance some indication of the policy that was to be proposed' (Wrigley, 1991, p. 63).

The stresses and strains of the Liberal relationship with Labour in office for two years in 1929–31 were to reveal unambiguously the divisions within the Liberal Party. While some of the Liberal Council group, who thoroughly approved of Philip Snowden's stern Gladstonian finance and of Henderson and MacDonald's foreign policy, made good their promises of support to the Labour Government, others increasingly looked to the Conservatives. Early in the Government's life, when Lloyd George had adopted a posture of judging each government measure on its merits, he opposed the Coal Bill which he deemed to combine 'the worst features of socialism and individualism without the redeeming features of either'. Even though this Bill ran contrary to previous Liberal policy, including *Coal and Power*, the Government survived because on three occasions in late 1929 and early 1930 eight or more Liberal MPs either supported the Government or abstained – including Maclean and a few of his associates (Wilson, 1966, pp. 356–8; Campbell, 1977, pp. 256–60).

However, as time went on Lloyd George increased his support for the Labour Government, publicly justifying this by saying that it was a lesser evil than a Conservative government. In reality, unwilling to face an early General Election, he and the Liberals were as much captives of Labour as had been the young Labour Party to the Liberals after the December 1910 General Election. In this circumstance Sir John Simon and others, who had not been opposed by Conservatives at the 1929 General Election, increasingly looked to the Conservatives and not to Labour for a political future. After the summer of 1930, when Lloyd George had been offering Labour greater co-operation in return for more Liberal-inclined policies on unemployment and agriculture plus legislation on electoral reform, Simon and four others voted with the Conservatives. By March 1931 Simon had abandoned Free Trade. In late June he, along with Ernest Brown and Sir Robert Hutchison (who had been Lloyd George's Chief Whip from November 1926 to November 1930), resigned the

131

Liberal Whip. This was just the most dramatic sign of division. Earlier, in March 1931, when Lloyd George pressed for general support for the Labour Government, although 33 MPs supported this, 19 had opposed it, either wishing to eject Labour or at least to stand aloof.

For Lloyd George the period of the second Labour Government was extremely frustrating, particularly because of its failure to adopt a dynamic response to rising unemployment. Lloyd George was happier with its performance on agriculture − especially from the time in June 1930 when his former close associate Christopher Addison became Minister of Agriculture and introduced a Land Utilization Bill and an Agricultural Marketing Bill. But as MacDonald and several of his senior colleagues appeared increasingly demoralized by the economic problems they faced, Lloyd George personally became more significant in the fortunes of the Labour Government. At the Liberal Party Conference on 17 October 1930 he had commented: 'It is all a question of who drives the coach. We propose to press for more expedition and determination' (Campbell, 1977, p. 275). By early 1931 Lloyd George was being consulted more frequently. George Lansbury, the authentic voice of the Labour Left, wrote (on his own authority) to Lloyd George in February 1931, urging him to join the Labour Party and even to become its deputy leader, with a few Cabinet seats for other Liberals who accompanied him. In late July 1931, just before the Labour Government collapsed in the economic crisis, it appears that MacDonald was seriously considering offering Lloyd George the Leadership of the House of Commons combined with the post of either Foreign Secretary or Chancellor of the Exchequer (Campbell, 1977, pp. 282−5, 293−4). Whether Lloyd George would have accepted is another matter. He was taken seriously ill on 27 July 1931 and needed a prostate operation. But later in the year he could reflect to his old friend and political associate, Sir Herbert Lewis: 'When I was struck down in the late summer we had complete control of the Parliamentary situation and the Labour government was getting more and more into our hands' (Wrigley, 1991, p. 68).

After the collapse of the second Labour Government Lloyd George's political influence was much reduced. Before this, for some nine years after his fall from office in October 1922 he had remained a major figure in British politics; indeed, there have been very large claims for his significance in these years. Kenneth O. Morgan has declared that 'it is clear that the politics of the 1920s were in large measure a reaction against Lloyd George, a reaction in which the

Conservative and Labour parties made common cause' (Morgan, 1974, p. 170). His views were endorsed and amplified by John Campbell who argued, 'It is not too much to say that the whole inter-war period was a conscious reaction against Lloyd George' and that 'the age of Baldwin and MacDonald in reality revolved around Lloyd George' (Campbell, 1977, pp. 3, 11). While it is certainly true that in the 1920s Baldwin and MacDonald loathed Lloyd George, it is the case that his more immediate impact on politics was at its height when politics were in a state of flux. This was so in the period from October 1922 to the General Election of 1923, when the lost Tory leaders might have drifted further away from their old party, as so many of the Peelites had done after 1846, and during the hung Parliaments of 1924 and 1929–31. Certainly, during Baldwin's second Government of 1924–9 Lloyd George hardly had a great direct impact on it (though, indirectly, the leaders of that Government did eschew his high profile and interventionist ways).

From 1931 Lloyd George was a statesman without a party. Whatever his prestige, he had only a handful of votes to deliver in the House of Commons. He was estranged from the bulk of his party between the 1931 and 1935 General Elections, though he and his family group of MPs took the Liberal Whip again after the 1935 General Election. He himself had harmed the Liberal Party's electoral chances soon after the 1929 General Election by cutting off the money from his political fund. The party received no more cash from him after June 1930 (Wilson, 1966, pp. 352–4). Hence the Liberal Party machine, previously made a supplicant to his whim, appeared almost a rich man's plaything. Worst of all, that man, Lloyd George, had become rich as a consequence of rising to prominence via the Liberal Party. The laying off of staff and the lack of funds to finance Liberal by-election candidates or 1931 General Election candidates aroused further great animosity towards Lloyd George. In the 1931 General Election there were only 160 Liberal candidates, compared to the 512 of 1929.

When in February 1931 Lloyd George replied to Lansbury's invitation to join the Labour Party, he had declared, 'Like yourself I am now merely concerned with spending the remainder of my life and strength in advancing ideas and causes which I was brought up to believe in.' This gives at least a partial description of his domestic political activities during the 1930s.

As always, he treated Free Trade as desirable, not as dogma. In 1933 he aroused a measure of controversy when he argued that, given the Government's determination to pursue a policy of Imperial Preference, there should be 'fair and equal treatment for the cultivators of the soil'. During the 1935 General Election he recognized that it was a dead issue. Frances Stevenson later noted in her diary:

> He is pleased with the Welsh results — sorry that one or two did not get in who might have done had they not clung to the fetish of free trade. One of them he advised to leave free trade alone. 'I must stick to my principles,' was the reply. 'Do you want to get to heaven or to Westminster?' was D.'s slightly cynical retort. (Taylor, 1971b, p. 319)

Lloyd George remained very much attached to his old causes of the land and agriculture. His interest in these matters was stimulated by his enjoyment of his own estate at Churt, where he drove his farm managers to distraction by his persistent interventions. During the 1930s and in the Second World War he spoke up for farmers, and increasingly saw himself as the natural spokesperson for the agrarian interest. In conversation at Churt in 1938 he told one acquaintance that the

> tragedy today was that there was no one in government who came from the land — you must be born and bred on it to understand it. Baldwin had admitted to him in the Smoking Room one day that he didn't possess a single pig —' in spite of the illusion that all he cared for was the country and his pigs. (Thomas Jones Papers, A2/39)

Drawing on his experience as Premier during the First World War, he often declared that agriculture would be a key industry in another war. At the time of the Anglo-German Naval Agreement in 1935 he condemned the Government's willingness to agree to Germany having 60 per cent of, or, if circumstances warranted, parity with the British fleet of submarines (Rowland, 1975, pp. 704, 706, 720).

He was also willing to take up the issue of unemployment again. In May 1933 Ernest Bevin sent him his booklet *My Plan for 2,000,000 Workers*. Lloyd George responded:

> It is very suggestive and courageous.
>
> We are not going to get out of this trouble until something on the lines you indicate is attempted. I particularly like your line on hours of labour and pensions for those who have reached 60. More power to your elbow. (Letter, 29 May 1933; Lloyd George Papers, G/3/10/3)

134

In 1934 he was approached by leading Welsh industrialists to produce a policy to relieve the economic depression in South Wales. This he organized at Churt with the help, as in the late 1920s, of Lord Lothian, Seebohm Rowntree and a team of experts. The end result was *What's Wrong with South Wales*, a reworked version of the Yellow Book aimed at the particular problems of South Wales, for which Lloyd George wrote the Preface. In it he declared:

> The force of habit, says Karl Marx somewhere, is stronger than the force of arms. You can get used to anything, to the figures of unemployment, for example, You can come to look upon two million idle men as part of the natural order, like a rainy day . . .
> This pamphlet is not a programme, except by implication. It is an attempt to sting the reader out of complacency. There is nothing 'inevitable' in the state of South Wales, Durham and Cumberland. Others have drawn up reports, programmes, plans in details. But the government is as lazy as it dares to be. We can stop the rot if we will to do so; if we don't, it will spread and we shall not escape.

By the time this pamphlet was published in the summer of 1935 Lloyd George was making a final attempt to mobilize the remaining forces of nonconformity and Liberal opinion in Britain to defeat MacDonald, Baldwin and the National Government. He was no longer the leader of the Liberal Party, but he still commanded the attention of the press and radio. Indeed, Frances Stevenson noted rather disparagingly of the South Wales research at its outset, 'Even if the net result is negligible, there is bound to be a vast amount of publicity!' (Taylor, 1971b, p. 283).

Lloyd George, as always, was very ready to make use of major nonconformist platforms. In 1933 he addressed the annual conference of the National Council of Free Churches and urged them to take action to deal with the 'great moral issue' of unemployment and also reflected on the way the Treaty of Versailles had been applied firmly to Germany but had been ignored by others. By late 1934 Lloyd George was willing to join with them in a campaign which stressed peace as well as reconstruction along the lines of the 1929 programmes and his own recent work on the problems of South Wales and the rest of the country. Hence in January 1935 Lloyd George launched an apparently non-party campaign on these issues; ostensibly, his 'primary concern was for the adoption of his programme, not for

135

office' (Koss, 1975, pp. 189–95). His memorandum *Organising Prosperity: A Scheme of National Reconstruction* was put to the Government.

MacDonald, Baldwin and their colleagues deliberately took their time to consider this memorandum. For a period it seemed possible that Lloyd George would be offered government office. But in the end the leaders of the National Government decided to keep their distance from him and his scheme. When this became apparent, Lloyd George did not await a formal rejection of his proposals but issued on 5 June 'A Call to Action'. Thereafter his Council of Action campaigned across Britain. But many leading nonconformists did not support it, neither was nonconformity the force it had been. W. P. Crozier, editor of the *Manchester Guardian*, noted after seeing Lloyd George, that 'he was assuming the existence of a "Nonconformist role" of the old kind. He had talked a great deal of what had happened in the days of Gladstone ... and seemed to think things had not changed.' In the November 1935 General Election the Council of Action had little or no impact, even though Lloyd George provided £400,000 from his political fund (Koss, 1975, pp. 204–5).

This was Lloyd George's last creative phase on domestic policy. As Kenneth O. Morgan has observed of his reformulation of the 1929 Liberal programmes:

> Many called it Britain's 'New Deal', adopting the name of Roosevelt's programmes in the United States at the time. But the main inspiration for the Council of Action lay clearly in the wartime policies pursued in Britain after 1915. (Morgan, 1974, p. 182)

Indeed, during the 1930s Lloyd George was reliving the years 1914–19, vindicating his wartime leadership and drawing various political lessons from those times as he wrote his *War Memoirs* (six volumes, 1933–6) and *The Truth about the Peace Treaties* (1938).

Between 1933 and 1935 Lloyd George continued to look both to the Left and to the Right for possible political openings, just as he had done in the 1920s. The 1935 campaign for peace and reconstruction had been a forlorn attempt to conjure up from the depths of the past the forces which had been the backbone of old Liberalism. Earlier, on 13 November 1934, he had discussed with Addison the possibility of an electoral deal with Labour at the next General Election. Frances Stevenson noted that 'D. thinks he can promise them a good dozen seats in Wales, and more in England, if Labour will give him a quid pro quo.' However, nine days later when he saw

George Lansbury, the Labour Party leader, the latter confessed that he doubted 'whether he could persuade his party to come to any sort of national agreement or agreement on a national policy' (Taylor, 1971b, pp. 290, 292).

Lloyd George consoled himself with the thought that 'he would rather come to terms with the Conservatives.' Younger radical Conservatives such as Harold Macmillan and Edward Grigg had been sounding him out since May 1934. Lloyd George, aware of the marginal nature of the parliamentary seats of Macmillan and some of his colleagues, was not that eager to help. As Frances Stevenson put it, 'He is not going to pull Tory chestnuts (even young ones) out of the fire for them' (Taylor, 1971b, p. 280). But between March and May 1935, when the Government was considering his 'New Deal' proposals, Lloyd George did consider the possibility of joining the National Government. However, as he made the removal of so many old enemies from their current posts in the Government a precondition (just as he was to do in 1940), it is difficult to judge how serious he really was in all this.

After the Government's rebuff to his memorandum *Organising Prosperity*, Lloyd George had hopes of another hung Parliament resulting from the next election. He and his nonconformist supporters would contribute to reducing the National Government's majority, or even to wiping it out. Then, in his day dreams, Lloyd George envisaged a return to power. On 17 July 1935 Frances Stevenson noted his aspirations, should there be an insufficient Labour and Liberal majority for a vigorous policy:

'Under those circumstances,' said D., 'I would form a government with Lansbury as nominal Prime Minister, but retaining the active leadership for myself. I would then proceed to formulate a devastating progressive programme and go to the country again immediately upon it with a terrific campaign, and return with a majority of 150.'   (Taylor, 1971b, p. 312)

Lloyd George made clear to Labour that he was not ideologically against collectivist measures, was amenable to public ownership of the land, the railways and electricity, and accepted that the 'ownership of the mines cannot be left where it is' (Rowland, 1975, p. 721). During the General Election campaign itself Sylvester noted, 'He is moving heaven and earth to get electors to vote Labour where there is no Liberal' (Cross, 1975, p. 134). However, his hopes and dreams of power were shattered when the National Government retained a large majority in the 1935 General Election.

Much of Lloyd George's political energy in the 1930s went into foreign affairs. He repeatedly drew on his own experiences as Premier to offer the government, the House of Commons and the country advice on the big issues of the day. At first he saw Hitler and the Nazis as a lesser evil than communism, though he did condemn, albeit without great vigour, the incarceration of their opponents in concentration camps and the attacks on Jews. As for Hitler himself he was initially outspoken in praise of him as a dynamic leader who had tackled unemployment by massive public works and who had stood up for German interests against unreasonable aspects of the Treaty of Versailles. In 1936 Lloyd George was a forthright appeaser of Hitler. This phase reached its nadir when he visited Hitler at Berchtesgaden on 4 and 5 September. They discussed international issues, agriculture and social measures. Of the last Lloyd George commented, 'Germany had always excelled', and went to talk with enthusiasm about Germany's approach to unemployment, health insurance, welfare organizations and leisure (Thomas Jones Papers, A2/34). He returned greatly impressed from his major interview with Hitler: '"He is a very great man," said L. G. "'Führer' is the proper name for him, for he is a born leader, yes, and statesman"' (Cross, 1975, p. 148).

While for some time Lloyd George admired Hitler, he never had any time for Mussolini. In this his attitude may have been partially coloured by his taste for adopting national stereotypes; the Greeks, for example, being esteemed more highly than Italians. In 1935 and 1936 he repeatedly attacked Baldwin and his colleagues for their failure to assist Abyssinia against Italian aggression. His devastating verbal onslaught on Baldwin on this issue in the Commons on 20 June 1936 was dubbed by Churchill 'one of the greatest Parliamentary performances of all time' (Taylor, 1971(b), p. 324).

However, with the Spanish Civil War, his attitude to Hitler changed. At first, Lloyd George had hopes that Hitler would keep out of involvement in Spain. During his longer meeting in September 1936 he had aired his disagreement with Hitler. In late 1937, in a letter probably intended to be shown to Hitler, he stated: 'Mussolini is temperamentally an aggressor. I have never thought that Herr Hitler was and I do not believe it now', before going on to reiterate his concern about German intervention in Spain. By this time, or at least by early 1938, his unease at Hitler's policy towards Spain was giving

138

way to distrust and also to concern that Neville Chamberlain's Government was not being firm with the dictators.

What Lloyd George particularly deplored was half-hearted measures, be they ineffective economic sanctions against Italy over Abyssinia or weakness when negotiating with Hitler. When Chamberlain recognized the Italian conquest of Abyssinia, Lloyd George complained in the Commons on 2 May 1938 that the dictators

> know that the government has no fight in them except in the House of Commons. ... They are quite convinced you won't fight. So am I. The Germans know it, and they are just looking at your record. Every time, after threatening, you withdraw, and this is one of the most abject, dishonourable, cowardly surrenders of all. Having promised protection to a weak nation, you sell it for your own peace of mind. Until we have a government that makes it quite clear that at one point it will stand − with the nation and Empire behind it − we shall not get peace in Europe. (Rowland, 1975, p. 750)

The Munich agreement of 30 September 1938 came as no surprise. But he did not speak out over the betrayal of Czechoslovakia for a month. Then he declared:

> Having urged the Czechoslovakian government to make concessions ... we handed over a little democratic state in central Europe, the land of John Huss, wrapped in a union jack and the tricolour, to a ruthless dictator, who will deny freedom to Czechs and Germans alike. We were not ready even to defend ourselves, let along rescue others. That is our only excuse for not standing up to the dictators, and history will ask but one question over that episode: 'Is incompetence a justification for bad faith?' (Cross, 1975, pp. 220−1)

By this time Lloyd George was in no doubt that Hitler was a greater threat than Stalin and communism. In a speech at Llandudno on 19 January 1939 Lloyd George warned: 'The supreme diplomatic imbecility of snubbing Russia ought to be repaired without loss of time. The peril is great − and it is imminent' (Aster, 1971, p. 338).

After Hitler had occupied the remaining part of Czechoslovakia in mid-March, Chamberlain gave unconditional guarantees to Poland and Romania without consulting Russia, let alone reaching an agreement with her. At his request, Lloyd George saw Chamberlain privately at the Commons on 31 January 1939. Lloyd George made

139

clear his view that Chamberlain's policy of an alliance with just France and Poland and reliance on an expectation 'that Russia would come in ultimately' was 'a very reckless gamble' (Cross, 1975, p. 225). Thereafter Lloyd George joined Churchill and the Labour Party in trying to push Chamberlain against his will towards an Anglo-Soviet alliance. When Chamberlain introduced a Bill for conscription in late April 1939 Lloyd George denounced the Government's 'demented pledges' to Poland, Romania and Greece, given the lack of an understanding with Russia, but voted for the Bill in spite of the Parliamentary Liberal Party's decision to abstain. Thereafter Lloyd George viewed the prospect of impending war with despondency.

Between the 1935 General Election and the outbreak of the Second World War Lloyd George's views still attracted political attention. His outspoken attacks on the Government's foreign policy won him many admirers across the political spectrum of the House of Commons. Several of the younger Conservative MPs consulted him, including Harold Macmillan, Robert Boothby and Brendan Bracken. Lloyd George also had good relations with many leading Labour figures, including those on the Left. Thus, in 1937 he tried to assist James Maxton in stopping the execution of POUM (*Partido Obrero de Unificación Marxista*, the United Marxist Workers' Party) prisoners by the Spanish government, and he also wrote to the officials of the Albert Hall urging them to lift a ban on Sir Stafford Cripps speaking there. On 1 March 1939 he was sufficiently moved by one of Attlee's attacks on the Government to send him a telegram which stated: 'Thrilled with your outspoken and courageous arraignment ... Time that egotistical humbug should be taken by the throat' (Lloyd George Papers, G/1/12/1).

But from the time of his seventy-fifth birthday in January 1938, Lloyd George's powers appeared to be declining noticeably. At times in the Commons he lost his fluency. He was increasingly nervous of making quick reactions to opponents. By early 1938 he was admitting that his office-holding days were over. On 14 March Sylvester noted in his diary:

> Tweed told me the other day that he had been talking about the general political situation with LG and the possibility of LG taking office in a Labour government. LG had said that he would never take office again. 'Fancy having to be in town every day, running a department, or in the House − it would kill me.' (Cross, 1975, p. 201)

140

However, the new political situation brought about by the war in Europe rekindled his aspirations. In 1940 he was perceived to be still capable of holding high office; that he did not take up offers from Churchill was due to a mix of reasons. Though he still craved attention, to be seen as one who still counted on the political stage and who could still share some political kudos with his personal political entourage, one reason he declined office was his own aware-ness of his declining faculties and the risk of appearing a failure. It was safer to stay aloof and criticize, to pronounce on the lessons of the First World War and to carp at Churchill's performance. But there were other reasons to do, at first, with distaste for the presence in the Government of Neville Chamberlain and others of the Old Gang, and with his belief that he might enter office at some later stage to rescue something for Britain from failed policies.

The essence of Lloyd George's fears of 1937–9 came true with the outbreak of war on 3 September 1939. Chamberlain had em-broiled Britain in a war with Germany without the support of either the Soviet Union or the USA. Unlike Chamberlain, he had never seen Poland as strong enough to be a military power threatening Germany with a second front in the east. But he deplored the British and French failure to help Poland. On 27 September Lloyd George complained to a meeting of MPs that Britain should have assisted Poland by immediately bombing German munitions factories. To Boothby he said:

We ought to be attacking. . . . Why aren't we attacking? If it is because they haven't got the stuff, they should never have given the guarantee to Poland. In the meantime Germany is producing far more arms than we. Delay only widens the gap.

He went on to suggest, 'This is a struggle for world power, in which aeroplanes are one weapon and diplomacy is another.' His conclusion appeared to be that Britain should achieve a negotiated peace, like the Treaty of Amiens in the Napoleonic Wars, and then construct a sufficiently powerful coalition against Germany (Addison, 1971, pp. 367–8; Rowland, 1975, pp. 762–3).

With the fall of Poland, Lloyd George saw even more reason to consider a negotiated peace. If neither the Soviet Union nor the USA joined Britain he saw no chance of victory. At the start of 1940 he told Hugh Cudlipp over lunch:

People call me a defeatist, but what I say to them is: Tell me how we can win! Can we win in the air? Can we win at sea,

141

when the effect of our naval blockade is wiped out by Germany's connections with Russia? How can we win on the land? The Germans cannot get through the Maginot Line: when do you think we can get through the Siegfried Line? (Rowland, 1975, p. 767)

Publicly he showed some caution in expressing such views. After he had suggested in the Commons on 3 October 1939 that if Germany offered peace terms Britain 'should not come to too hurried a conclusion', his view had been firmly disavowed by most leading politicians. Even his faithful secretary Sylvester had been shocked, noting in his diary, 'I could read more into that speech than most people, for I know his mind, which is far in advance of what he said.' When he prepared a similar speech for a public meeting in his constituency, his daughter Megan expressed her distaste for the 'passages which give a defeatist attitude' (Cross, 1975, pp. 238, 241). However, at the meeting in Carnarvon on 21 October, facing a crowd of 6–9,000 people, he abandoned many such passages. Sylvester wrote of his speech:

One moment he was playing up to the blue-blooded Tories – and many were present – talking about our superb air force and about the greatest navy in the world; you could feel them puff with pride. Next he was playing up to the peacemongers, by advocating a conference and peace. Next he was giving a recital of intimate facts, not before stated, regarding our relations with Russia. The burden of his speech was really to influence the government to bring in Russia on our side, and to send a highly placed minister to see Stalin. (Cross, 1975, p. 242)

During early 1940 Lloyd George's interventions in Parliament were mostly about agriculture, a subject on which he had no difficulty in taking a positive line. Between February and April 1940 he made four speeches urging immediate action for an expansion of arable farming comparable to that which had taken place in 1917–18. On 13 March he warned:

It is no use starting a big programme of agriculture when the grim spectre of hunger has just appeared above the horizon. It must be done now ... I do not know what is happening about peace negotiations, but ... it would be a very fatal error for any goverment not to contemplate the possibility of a very long war. (Rowland, 1975, pp. 767–8)

142

Perhaps during the first four to five months of the year he was awaiting what to him was the inevitable replacement of Neville Chamberlain. Apparently, when he had seen Churchill on 14 December 1939, Churchill had promised to try to get him into government office when changes occurred (Cross, 1975, pp. 244–5).

Chamberlain's downfall came after the withdrawal of most of the British forces from Norway in early May. Lloyd George played a famous part in the undermining of Chamberlain in the House of Commons. He had been undecided about whether to speak in the debate, but he made up his mind to do so when Megan told him that Chamberlain had unwisely defied criticism by indicating that he would rely on the Whips to ensure his support (Foot, 1976, pp. 180–2). He ended a vigorous attack on the premier with what became famous words:

> He has appealed for sacrifice. The nation is prepared for every sacrifice so long as it has leadership, so long as the government show clearly what they are aiming at and so long as the nation is confident that those who are leading it are doing their best. I say solemnly that the Prime Minister should give an example of sacrifice, because there is nothing which can contribute more to victory in this war than he should sacrifice the seals of office.

After Churchill took office on 10 May he delayed over a fortnight before making an offer to Lloyd George. Then the position of Director of Food Production was made, subject to Chamberlain's agreement. By 4 June, when Churchill had Chamberlain's agreement and made Lloyd George a firm offer, the latter had decided to decline. Lloyd George's decision was undoubtedly assisted by his unwillingness to serve with Chamberlain. He also took umbrage at the slowness and conditional nature of the offer; he may even have had hopes of a place in the War Cabinet of five. These were his main reasons, together perhaps with his doubts about his physical resilience. If at this time he saw a bigger role for himself in the future, it was in daydreams of being a British Clemenceau.

After Marshal Pétain signed an armistice with Germany on 22 June, Lloyd George's closest associates feared that he was giving the impression of being willing to be a British Pétain. Lloyd George remained impressed by Hitler and doubtful that Britain could break his army. Indeed, part of the reason for Lloyd George's gloom was that he kept looking back to the First World War and its massive battles, and was concerned that Britain was not 'getting to grips' with

143

the German army. However, he felt that a negotiated peace could only be considered from a position of some strength. On 14 September 1940 he informed the Duke of Bedford that it was the wrong time to start any movement for such negotiations. 'Were we to make peace overtures now whilst the threat of invasion was impending over our heads, it would be stigmatised as a Pétain move inspired by fear of utter defeat' (Rowland, 1975, p. 779). Nine days later Frances Stevenson observed, 'L. G. has some idea he is coming in on the peace settlement, that he will be able to make peace where Winston won't' (Cross, 1975, p. 279). In seeing the possible need for such a settlement if neither the Soviet Union nor the USA entered the war, Lloyd George was not unique. As Paul Addison has commented, 'He represented, outside the government, the same kind of policy as Halifax and [R. A.] Butler represented inside' (Addison, 1971, p. 381).

When Lord Lothian, the British Ambassador in Washington, died on 14 December 1940, Lloyd George was offered the post. He was delighted to be the centre of attention again, but had little hesitation in declining. Lord Dawson of Penn, who gave him a medical examination, wrote him a letter which stated that he was 'sound in wind and limb' but went on to state:

> From a medical point of view you could take a post involving policy though not one involving heavy administration.
> On account of the particular strains attaching to such a post, I would advise you not to accept Washington. (Lloyd George Papers, G/6/4/12)

Churchill, who saw him to discuss the post, afterwards commented that Lloyd George had aged markedly even in the few months since he had offered him government office.

Lloyd George continued to age fast in 1941. He received a major blow to his morale when his wife died on 20 January. In spite of his close attachment to Frances Stevenson and his occasional affairs with other women, Lloyd George had remained emotionally linked to Margaret throughout her life. To Churchill and others who gave their condolences he observed, 'She was a great pal in a stormy life.' After a decent interval – and in spite of Megan's vehement opposition – he married Frances Stevenson on 23 October 1943.

From 1941 until his death Lloyd George remained querulous and critical of the conduct of the war. His private talk in October 1940 that 'I shall wait until Winston is bust' was just talk. In 1941 he still

144

saw a role for himself as 'England's "last chance" as a negotiator' (Cross, 1975, p. 281; Rowland, 1975, p. 785). However, in the Commons on 19 December 1940 he did make encouraging comments following Italian setbacks and on 3 April 1941, when calling again for a more dynamic agricultural policy, he rejoiced in the 'series of the most brilliant victories on land, at sea and in the air that have ever illuminated the military annals of this country'. When he criticized the Government's conduct of the war on 7 May 1941 he made some telling points on food output, air-raid shelters, and blunders of policy over Greece and North Africa; though he ended on what had become an obsession: the need for Churchill to have 'a small war council who will help him ... in counsel, ... advice and ... in action' (367 *H. C. Deb. 5s*, c.1409; 370 *H. C. Deb. 5s*, c.1235; 371 *H. C. Deb. 5s*, c.879−81).

In 1942 Lloyd George took interest in post-war reconstruction. Tom Jones noted in August:

> I've had several political talks with L. G. He's more pro-Eden than pro-Cripps at the moment. Also much interested in the Reconstruction Committee, and wants a ginger group to push it ... (Thomas Jones Papers, A1/49)

He took particular interest in Beveridge's plans. After he had seen Beveridge, Frances Stevenson wrote on 6 March 1942 to ask if he 'could outline to him in greater detail the plans you mentioned or the abolition of want after the war' (Lloyd George Papers, G/3/9/5). When there was a vote in the Commons over the Government's reluctance fully to accept the Beveridge Report, Lloyd George was among those opposing the Government.

Lloyd George was delighted when Russia entered the war. His last significant speech in the Commons was on 11 June 1942 when he welcomed the treaty of alliance with the Soviet Union. He observed, 'Had it been a fact some years ago many blunders in foreign policy would have been avoided. Not only that: this war could never have occurred.' He was to urge Britain and the USA to open up a second front in Europe without delay. Appropriately, his last visit to the Commons was on D-Day, 6 June 1944, to hear Churchill formally announce that the landings in Europe had taken place.

Lloyd George, terminally ill with cancer, left Churt to return to Llanystumdwy on 19 September 1944. In a final speech in Carnarvon on 9 November he spoke of the victory soon to come and of the problems of peace-making. Even at this stage of his life, he still hoped to have a part to play in the post-war discussions on peace. By this time he was not fit to fight another General Election and his local agent advised that he could not be sure of winning if he did. On these grounds he became willing to accept an earldom. This was announced in the 1945 New Year Honours List. He took the title of Earl Lloyd-George of Dwyfor and Viscount Gwynedd. This was a strange end to his career. As late as October 1936 he had been commenting on the wisdom of Gladstone, Bright, Cobden, Labouchere and Joseph Chamberlain in not taking honours (Cross, 1975, p. 158). But the dying Lloyd George still had hopes of a final entry into the political limelight. He died in the evening of 26 March 1945 and was buried in a plot he had selected by the Dwyfor on the edge of Llanystumdwy.

# 7

## *The Welsh Wizard*

Lloyd George's personality has proved elusive to so many historians and biographers. He was a man of rapidly changing moods, varying quickly from jaunty humour to pathos and from intimacy to that of man-of-the-world reconteur. His politics, too, did not fit a simple pattern – or at least not one familiar to those who grew up in the period after his death.

Lloyd George has often been compared to Joseph Chamberlain, yet a notable feature of Lloyd George's career is that he did not linger long in the Tory embrace. Indeed, for most of the time that he worked in association with Tories (1916–22 out of 1915–23) he was Prime Minister and they were maintaining him in power, even though he had to perform great feats of political agility to stay that long at the top of the greasy pole. Of these years in which he depended on Tory support, up until the Irish settlement of December 1921 or even up to the Genoa conference of April–May 1922, Lloyd George can have felt he was still making a notable political contribution in office. From the time of the 1923 General Election he resumed a leadership role in the Liberal Party, and his involvement was marked by his receptivity to new and radical ideas and by his sponsorship of major policy reviews.

Unlike Chamberlain, Lloyd George was not a wealthy businessman. He may have regretted this. Certainly he was always prone to idealize 'captains of industry'. During his first decade in the House of Commons, as an impecunious back-bencher in the period before the payment of MPs, he looked with envy at the money that apparently dull-witted Tory and Liberal MPs made from investments, and he indulged with a notable lack of success in South American speculations (Grigg, 1973, pp. 178–97). His personal finances improved when he achieved ministerial office from December 1905. Yet in 1912, when Chancellor of the Exchequer, he rashly joined Rufus Isaacs and Alexander Murray (soon to be the Master of Elibank) in speculating in American Marconi shares. Again he failed to make his fortune; but this time he jeopardized his career, as a major political scandal blew up in 1912–13 over what appeared to be insider dealing in shares and what was an attempt to mislead the House of Commons on this subject. Lloyd George's share-dealing was no worse than that done by several other ministers of both main political parties. Bentley Gilbert has observed, 'Lloyd George in purely financial terms was the victim, not the beneficiary, of private information', and has suggested that on the financial issue he was culpable 'only of avarice and ignorance'. His greater sin was to try to cover up the matter (Donaldson, 1962; Grigg, 1985, pp. 44–66; Searle, 1987, pp. 172–95; Gilbert, 1989).

To aspire to a comfortable life on the basis of lucrative investments was not unknown to nineteenth-century radicals nor, indeed, to twentieth-century Labour politicians. Lloyd George did not hide his taste for many of the contemporary enjoyments of the wealthy, such as motoring in continental Europe, golf and living in ample accommodation (in his case at Churt in Surrey, from 1922). Of this Hankey noted in his diary in May 1920: 'Altogether I had rather a disagreeable feeling that the PM is getting too fond of high living and I found Philip Kerr shared my feelings, though I am bound to say that we argued that though he likes it, he doesn't miss it if he has not got it' (Hankey Papers, 1/5, f.124). For all this, Lloyd George never shared Asquith's taste for country-house parties and London society. Yet Lloyd George's growing fondness for good living did not render hypocritical his expressions of social concern. They highlighted the fact that his social programme was aimed at uplifting those most in need, not at bringing about a social revolution. The fiery speeches that had made his name as an advanced radical were aimed at the landed interest, not at the propertied in general, and least of all at the middle classes.

Lloyd George's commitment to the tenets of Liberalism was often doubted at the time and subsequently. It is not hard to show that his support for major Liberal issues at various times was equivocal, be they Free Trade or Home Rule. Yet overall one of the clearest threads in his career was the location of his politics within the broad church of Liberalism. He often felt that Liberal notions were not perfect, but he repeatedly asserted that they were less imperfect than what was on offer from the Conservatives or Labour.

Lloyd George was born 25 years into Queen Victoria's long reign and his politics stemmed from the high Gladstonian period just before the Liberal divisions over Home Rule. His political advancement owed everything to his own endeavours. He was no landed grandee given prominence in his party because of his social status. He came from a relatively humble home, steeped in nonconformist and Liberal attitudes. His rise in the Liberal Party began as a grass-roots politician who operated skilfully within many of the pressure groups of Wales and nonconformist England. Lloyd George, like Winston Churchill, was a full-time politician.

Lloyd George graduated from pressure-group politics to coaxing the press or blatantly manipulating it. He had early become an adroit user of the local press. Once established at Westminster he worked equally hard at influencing editors of the national press, even arranging the purchase of major newspapers. Thus he spent his leisure hours with newspaper owners such as Sir George Riddell (*News of the World*) and Beaverbrook (*Daily Express*), took considerable pains to maintain the friendship of C. P. Scott, editor of the *Manchester Guardian*, put Beaverbrook, Northcliffe (owner of *The Times* and *Daily Mail*) and Rothermere (owner of the *Daily Mirror* and *Sunday Pictorial*) into government posts during the First World War, and during his premiership he showered peerages and other honours on newspaper owners and editors. Though he himself was not wealthy, on two notable occasions he mobilized wealthy Liberals to buy up newspapers. In 1901 the purchase of the *Daily News* was followed by its transformation overnight from being a pro-war Liberal newspaper into an anti-war one. Similarly, in 1918 the pro-Asquith *Daily Chronicle* was acquired and became the loyal supporter of Lloyd George and the Coalition Liberals. In the summer of 1922 he even considered getting together a consortium to buy *The Times* and to make him its editor. Of this A. J. P. Taylor has observed, 'The editor of *The Times* has often thought himself more important than the prime minister. Lloyd George was the only prime minister who apparently shared the belief' (Taylor, 1965, p. 187).

While he was a skilful at political manoeuvring and adroit at securing publicity for himself, a major element in his success was his powers of oratory. The historian can read great numbers of his speeches – but it is not easy, if at all possible, to recover his sense of timing, the delicate inflexion in his delivery, the accompanying gestures of head and hand. He was no ranter. On major occasions he delivered well-constructed, well-thought-out speeches, often building -up to an emotional climax. Into their preparation he put much emotional energy. Shortly before he gave his Queen's Hall speech of 19 September 1914 in favour of the war, Riddell noted of him:

> He was terribly nervous, feeling, he said, as if he were about to be executed. It was a curious sight to see him lying on the sofa, yawning and stretching himself in a state of high nervous excitement. (Riddell, 1933a, p. 32)

A. J. Sylvester, who worked for Lloyd George as his private secretary from 1919 to 1945, later commented:

> Often LG would start to prepare for an important speech many days in advance. He would dictate it. Finally he would skeletonise it, so that when he appeared on the platform he would have only the outlines of his speech before him. He was always at his best when − after mastering his subject, in which he took endless pains, with only skeletonised notes or with none at all − he relied on the atmosphere of the occasion for inspiration to put his thoughts into words. (Notes, February 1948; Thomas Jones Papers, AZ/40)

Lloyd George was equally careful in the presentation of his speeches. He often spoke softly at first, in order to encourage his audience to listen carefully. His gestures were well thought out − for example, with the thrusting out of a hand to highlight the words which followed, not the other way round. Harold Macmillan later recalled the advice Lloyd George gave him:

> there must be continual variation; slow solemn phrases, quick, witty amusing passages. Above all say to yourself as you get up, 'Vary the pace and vary the pitch.' This is the heart of the whole matter. Finally, don't forget the value of the 'pause'. (Macmillan, 1975, p. 58)

It is even less easy to recreate his personal magnetism which he could turn on to affect even the most hostile or suspicious persons with whom he was negotiating. He succeeded in mixing charm and threats to good effect even with groups who, when they set out to see him, were very determined to resist all his blandishments. Among several famous instances of this were his dealings with Smillie and the Miners Federation of Great Britain at the time of the setting-up of the Sankey Commission in February 1919 and with the Irish delegates in December 1921. An early impression of his skills, recorded later by a Tory MP and railway director, Sir Herbert Maxwell, relates to the threatened railway dispute of 1907:

> On the morning of the day arranged for our meeting with Lloyd George, we held a preliminary meeting at Euston Station, where it was unanimously resolved that we would not yield in the slightest degree to any proposal that he might put forward inconsistent with our determination to deal direct with our men, without intervention by the unions.
>
> Down we went to the Board of Trade and were received by the President, affable in manner, slight in person, and, as we thought, amateurish in expression. Before any one spoke on our side, Lloyd George addressed us at length. He displayed such a thorough acquaintance with all the ins and outs of the subject; such a reasonable sympathy with the aspirations of the men; dwelt so forcibly on the disastrous consequences to the country of a prolonged strike on the railways, pointing out how, without compromising our authority, he thought we might set up machinery for settling domestic difficulties, that our opposition melted away and we left the conference having consented to the appointment of conciliation boards or committees.

Though Maxwell's memory conflates several meetings, it is a representative account of Lloyd George as a negotiator. Indeed, one can go further, and point to him doing similar with the railwaymen, coaxing them into an agreement which they later regretted (Wrigley, 1976, p. 56).

Lloyd George also turned on his charm with women with frequent success. He would focus all his attention on a woman, make great efforts to understand and sympathize with the way she was thinking, and provide a sympathetic ear and good-humoured companionship, albeit often briefly. Ella Hepworth Dixon (the daughter of a popular historian and biographer) recalled:

> Socially, Mr Lloyd George is extraordinarily attractive. He has great charm. Always seizing the merest hint of a joke, you need never 'explain' anything to this twinkly-eyed Celt of outstanding personality. (Dixon, 1930, p. 198)

Indeed, his warmth and humour, his energy and zest for life, made

151

him a memorable companion. Sir Arthur Salter, a leading civil servant, noted after one of Lloyd George's breakfast parties:

> He was in his best form. ... He convulsed us all with one tale after another. When he paused for a moment, Mrs Lloyd George, with tears running down her face with laughter, turned to me and said, 'You wouldn't think I should laugh so at his jokes after all these years, would you? But I can't help it.' (Rowland, 1975, p. 228)

Lloyd George enjoyed company − or at least, he enjoyed the company of witty and outgoing people, weighty but not pompous politicians and journalists, and attractive women. The stories are legion of Lloyd George discomfiting the self-important, and this irreverence was part of his charm. Thus, in October 1918 Hankey noted in his diary that he had told such a Lloyd George tale to Arthur Balfour:

> The story was that a great American newspaper magnate was brought down to Walton Heath on a Sunday night to see Lloyd George. Instead of hearing words of wisdom on the political situation, all he had was a gramophone playing Welsh hymns and Lloyd George singing the bass part. Balfour laughed so much that all the people in the road stopped to watch and laughed too. (Hankey Papers, HNKY 1/5/31)

Beaverbrook, when comparing Britain's leaders in the two world wars, was to give the verdict, 'Churchill was perhaps the greater man but George was more fun' (Taylor, introduction to Morgan, 1974, p. 7). Similarly Bonar Law, even before the First World War, could remark: 'Lloyd George is a dangerous rascal, but a charming man, unspoilt by success' (Riddell, 1934, p. 122).

Lloyd George's liveliness in good company and the way he responded to others, using his powers of discerning others' anxieties and desires, made some contemporaries wonder what there was of him when alone. Keynes, writing just after the 1919 Paris Peace Conference, when his view of Lloyd George was at its lowest, made the chilling asssessment.

> Lloyd George is rooted in nothing; he is void and without content; he lives and feeds on his immediate surroundings; he is an instrument and a player at the same time which plays on the company and is played on by them too; he is a prism, as I

have heard him described, which collects light and distorts it and is most brilliant if the light comes from many quarters at once; a vampire and a medium in one. (Keynes, 1933, p. 36)

But while this has truth within it — notably that Lloyd George fed on situations and on those around him — it is too harsh.

There is greater perception in the assessment of Thelma Cazalet-Keir, a friend of Megan Lloyd George and later a left-wing Conservative MP. In 1920 she wrote of Lloyd George:

he is a complex character, but so is everyone to a certain degree. But he is extra-many sided; and that is why the average person who is only two- or three-sided himself finds it hard to understand a man who has at least a dozen different sides to his nature. He is the most sincere and insincere man I have ever met; he is the most honest and dishonest man I have ever met; he is the most grateful and ungrateful man I have ever met ... he is a man of the moment — I don't believe he ever really looks back or looks forward. That is why he is nearly always so full of vitality and happiness. When he is distressed, it only lasts a short time and is then forgotten. (Cazalet-Keir, 1967, pp. 49–50)

Lloyd George, indeed, displayed so often a 'live now pay later' or 'let tomorrow look after itself' attitude both to his affairs with women and to politics. He appeared to be at peace with himself enjoying short affairs with other women while still valuing and desiring to hold on to his relationships with Margaret, his first wife, and Frances Stevenson, eventually his second wife. In politics his concern to square problems in the present and avoid wasting intellectual energy in worrying about possible future repercussions was often a great source of strength. At least in the short term.

But in politics commitments that he gave to ease a present crisis often became future liabilities. Moreover, Lloyd George became adept at phrasing his promises so that the impression of what was on offer was stronger than what was defined by his exact wording. In time his Houdini-like skills at extricating himself from apparently cast-iron pledges made under duress reduced faith in his word. Moreover, his personal magnetism in negotiations did not carry on long enough after negotiations had ended to shield his reputation when one side learned that what he had promised them was somewhat different from what he had agreed with the other side. This was the case with many of his famous negotiations, from the 1907 railway dispute onwards.

Lloyd George also added to a reputation for deviousness by his taste for approaching political problems by indirect routes. As he put it, 'I never believed in costly frontal attacks either in war or politics, if there were a way round' (Lloyd George, 1934, p. 2274). Eventually his overall reputation for guile and chicanery undermined his chances of returning to office after 1922. Stanley Baldwin, who abhorred Lloyd George's style of politics, in the 1929 General Election applied to him a wounding dictum originally made by Thomas Carlyle: 'He spent his whole life in plastering together the true and the false, and therefrom manufacturing the plausible' (M. Gilbert, 1968, p. 122).

Yet the most wounding attacks made on Lloyd George as a politician have to do with his means rather than his ends. A. J. P. Taylor wrote, perhaps too generously, of Lloyd George's ending of intervention in Russia: 'As often happened with him, he had pursued a wise policy by methods of intrigue and evasion, and people remembered the methods but not the results' (*Observer*, 8 December 1968). Lloyd George failed to realize just how damaging his means were to his reputation. Indeed, given his efforts to destroy the Asquithians politically and his use of the Black and Tans in Ireland, Thelma Cazalet-Keir's account of his mood after the Irish Treaty of December 1921 highlights a remarkable blind spot in his outlook:

> The fact that it did not reverse nor even arrest the decline of the Coalition brought on an unusual fit of depression. ... He had expected that the Irish Treaty might have produced some pleasure among the Asquithians — but not! Not a glimmer! (Cazalet-Keir, 1967, pp. 63–4)

Lloyd George failed to realize that others were less prone than he to forget past ills quickly.

By 1922 his political methods had much devalued his considerable achievements. Yet, as F. S. Oliver observed at the end of the First World War when paying testimony to the 'imagination and enthusiasm combined with tremendous courage' that Lloyd George had displayed:

> People talk a great deal about his faults. Well, he has probably bigger faults than any other prominent politician; but you must expect a man's faults to be on a scale with his virtues. (M. Gilbert, 1968, p. 108)

In personal terms, he is often depicted as a man who 'went wrong' when he left the simple but worthy values of Llanystumdwy and Criccieth. Yet in a sense his life marked a continuous struggle along lines that had been laid out by Uncle Lloyd. His uncle had taught him the merits of self-help and had encouraged him in the expectation that others in his family would be self-sacrificing in supporting his progress up the social scale. On his daughter Olwen's tenth birthday Lloyd George wrote:

> The most pleasant thing in life is to feel that you are 'getting on'. Don't forget that. It is worth ten times more in happiness than wealth and grand things. Now getting on depends entirely on you yourself. Buck up Llwyd bach. (Letter, 2 April 1902; National Library of Wales, 20474C)

Lloyd George exceeded even his wildest ambitions. He did progress from Welsh cottage to 10 Downing Street.

# Bibliography

The archive collections cited are located as follows:

Hankey Papers: Churchill College, Cambridge
Lothian Papers: Scottish Record Office, Edinburgh
Simon Papers: Bodleian Library, Oxford.

The remainder are all in the National Library of Wales, Aberystwyth:

Ellis Papers; Ellis Griffiths Papers; S. T. Evans Papers; Thomas Jones Papers; J. H. Lewis Papers; Rendel Papers.

Adams, R. Q., 1978: *Arms and the Wizard.* London: Cassell.
Adams, R. Q. and Poirier, P., 1987: *The Conscription Controversy in Great Britain, 1900–1918.* London: Macmillan.
Addison, P., 1971: Lloyd George and compromise peace in the Second World War. In Taylor, 1971(a).
Asquith, M., 1920 and 1922: *The Autobiography of Margot Asquith.* London: Thornton Butterworth.
——, 1943: *Off the Record.* London: Frederick Muller.
Aster, S., 1971: Ivan Maisky and parliamentary anti-appeasement, 1938–39. In Taylor, 1971(a).
Beaverbrook, Lord, 1925: *Politicians and the Press.* London: Hutchinson.
——, 1928 and 1932: *Politicians and the War,* 2 vols. London: Thornton Butterworth and Lane.
——, 1956: *Men and Power.* London: Hutchinson.
——, 1963; *The Decline and Fall of Lloyd George.* London: Collins.
Bebbington, D. W., 1982: *The Nonconformist Conscience.* London: Allen & Unwin.
Bellamy, R. (ed.), 1990: *Victorian Liberalism.* London: Routledge.
Bentley, M., 1977: *The Liberal Mind, 1914–1929.* Cambridge: Cambridge University Press.

——, 1987: *The Climax of Liberal Politics*. London: Edward Arnold.

Bernstein, G. L., 1986: *Liberalism and Liberal Politics in Edwardian England*. London: Allen & Unwin.

Blake, R., 1966: *Disraeli*. London: Eyre & Spottiswoode.

Blake, R. (ed.), 1952: *The Private Papers of Douglas Haig, 1914–1919*. London: Eyre & Spottiswoode.

Blewett, N., 1972: *The Peers, the Parties and the People: the General Elections of 1910*. London: Macmillan.

Bourne, J. M., 1989: *Britain and the Great War, 1914–1918*. London: Edward Arnold.

Boyce, D. G., 1971: How to settle the Irish Question: Lloyd George and Ireland, 1916–21. In Taylor, 1971(a).

——, 1972: *Englishmen and Irish Troubles*. Cambridge, Mass.: MIT Press.

Brett, M. V. and Oliver, Viscount Esher, 1934 and 1938: *Journals and Letters of Reginald Viscount Esher*, 4 vols. London: Nicolson & Watson.

Brown, K. D., 1971: *Labour and Unemployment, 1900–1914*. Newton Abbot: David & Charles.

Brown, K. D. (ed.), 1974: *Essays in Anti-Labour History*. London: Macmillan.

——, 1985: *The First Labour Party*. London: Croom Helm.

Bunbury, H. N. (ed.), 1957: *Lloyd George's Ambulance Wagon: the memoirs of W. J. Braithwaite, 1911–1912*. London: Methuen.

Burk, K. (ed.), 1982: *War and the State*. London: Allen & Unwin.

Butler, D. (ed.), 1978: *Coalitions in British Politics*. London: Macmillan.

Campbell, J., 1975: The renewal of Liberalism: Liberalism without Liberals. In Peele and Cook, 1975.

——, 1977: *Lloyd George: the goat in the wilderness, 1922–1931*. London: Jonathan Cape.

——, 1983: *F. E. Smith*. London: Jonathan Cape.

Cazalet-Keir, T., 1967: *From the Wings*. London: Bodley Head.

'Centurion', 1923: *The Man Who Didn't Win the War: an exposure of Lloyd Georgism*. London: National Review.

Churchill, R. S., 1967: *Winston S. Churchill*, vol. 2. London: Heinemann.

Churchill, W. S., 1929: *The Aftermath*. London: Thornton Butterworth.

Clarke, P., 1978: *Liberals and Social Democrats*. Cambridge: Cambridge University Press.

Clarke, T., 1939: *My Lloyd George Diary*. London: Methuen.

Cline, P., 1974: Eric Geddes and the 'experiment' with businessmen in government, 1915–22. In Brown, 1974.

——, 1982: Winding down the war economy. In Burk, 1982.

Cowling, M. (1971): *The Impact of Labour, 1920–1924*. Cambridge: Cambridge University Press.

Cregier, D. M., 1976: *Bounder from Wales: Lloyd George's career before the First World War*. Columbia: University of Missouri Press.

——, 1982: *Chiefs without Indians*. Washington, DC: University Press of America.

157

Cross, C., 1975: *Life with Lloyd George: the diary of A. J. Sylvester*. London: Macmillan.

Dangerfield, G., 1935: *The Strange Death of Liberal England*. London: Constable.

Darwin, J., 1981: *Britain, Egypt and the Middle East*. London: Macmillan.

Davenport, N., 1974: *Memoirs of a City Radical*. London: Weidenfeld & Nicolson.

David, E., 1970: The Liberal Party divided, 1916–1918. *Historical Journal*, 13, 509–32.

David, E. (ed.), 1977: *Inside Asquith's Cabinet*. London: John Murray.

Davies, A. T., 1948: *The Lloyd George I Knew*. London: Henry Walter.

Davies, Sir Joseph, 1951: *The Prime Minister's Secretariat, 1916–1920*. Newport, Mon.: Johns.

Davies, J. Tafionydd, 1910: *D. Lloyd George*. Carmarthen: W. M. Evans.

Davies, W. Watkin, 1939: *Lloyd George, 1863–1914*. London: Constable.

Dingle, A. E., 1980: *The Campaign for Prohibition in Victorian England*. London: Croom Helm.

Dixon, E. H., 1930: *As I Knew Them*. London: Hutchinson.

Dockrill, M., 1971: David Lloyd George and foreign policy before 1914. In Taylor, 1971(a).

Dockrill, M. and Goold, J. D., 1981: *Peace without Promise: Britain and the peace conferences, 1919–1923*. London: Batsford.

Donaldson, F., 1962: *The Marconi Scandal*. London: Hart-Davis.

Douglas, R., 1971: *A History of the Liberal Party, 1895–1970*. London: Sidgwick & Jackson.

——, 1974: God gave the land to the people. In Morris, 1974.

——, 1976: *Land, People and Politics*. London: Allison & Busby.

Du Parcq, H., 1912–13: *Life of David Lloyd George*, 4 vols. London: Caxton.

Dutton, D., 1985: *Austen Chamberlain*. Bolton: Ross Anderson.

——, 1991: Lloyd George, Sir John Simon and the politics of the Liberal Party, 1919–31. In Loades, 1991.

Edwards, J. Hugh, 1913: *David Lloyd George*, 4 vols. London: Waverley Book Co.

Egerton, G. W., 1988: The Lloyd George *War Memoirs*: a study in the politics of memory. *Journal of Modern History*, 60, 55–94.

Ehrman, J., 1961: Lloyd George and Churchill as war leaders, *Transactions of the Royal Historical Society*, 11, 101–16.

Elcock, H., 1972: *Portrait of a Decision*. London: Eyre Methuen.

Emy, H. V., 1971: The Land Campaign: Lloyd George as a social reformer, 1909–14. In Taylor, 1971(a).

——, 1973: *Liberals, Radicals and Social Politics, 1892–1914*. Cambridge: Cambridge University Press.

Evans, B. G., n.d. [1916]: *The Life Romance of Lloyd George*. London: Everyman.

Evans, Olwen Carey, 1985: *Lloyd George Was My Father*. Llandysul: Gomer.

Fair, J. D., 1980: *British Interparty Conferences*. Oxford: Clarendon Press.

Fink, C., 1984: *The Genoa Conference*. Chapel Hill: University of North Carolina Press.

Foot, D., 1976: *British Political Crises*. London: Kimber.

Fraser, D., 1973: *The Evolution of the British Welfare State*. London: Macmillan.

Fraser, P., 1982: British war policy and the crisis of Liberalism in May 1915. *Journal of Modern History*, 52, 1–26.

Freeden, M., 1978: *The New Liberalism*. London: Oxford University Press.

——, 1986: *Liberalism Divided*. London: Oxford University Press.

——, 1990: The new Liberalism and its aftermath. In Bellamy, 1990.

French, D., 1986: *British Strategy and War Aims, 1914–1916*. London: Allen & Unwin.

——, 1988(a): Allies, rivals and enemies: British strategy and war aims during the First World War. In Turner, 1988.

——, 1988(b): The meaning of attrition, 1914–1916. *English Historical Review*, 103, 385–405.

Fry, M. G., 1977: *Lloyd George and Foreign Policy*, vol. 1. Montreal: McGill-Queen's University Press.

——, 1988: Political change in Britain, August 1914 to December 1916: Lloyd George replaces Asquith. *Historical Journal*, 31, 609–27.

Gardiner, A. G., 1908: *Prophets, Priests and Kings*. London: Dent.

——, 1913: *Pillars of Society*. London: Dent.

——, 1915: *The War Lords*. London: Dent.

——, 1923: *The Life of Sir William Harcourt*, 2 vols. London: Constable.

Garside, W. R., 1990: *British Unemployment, 1919–1939*. Cambridge: Cambridge University Press.

George, W., 1958: *My Brother and I*. London: Eyre & Spottiswoode.

George, W. R. P., 1976: *The Making of Lloyd George*. London: Faber & Faber.

——, 1983: *Lloyd George: backbencher*. Llandysul: Gomer.

Gilbert, B. B., 1966: *The Evolution of National Insurance in Great Britain*. London: Michael Joseph.

——, 1970: *British Social Policy, 1914–1939*. London: Batsford.

——, 1987: *David Lloyd George: the architect of change, 1863–1912*. London: Batsford.

——, 1989: David Lloyd George and the great Marconi scandal. *Historical Research*, 62, 295–317.

Gilbert, M. (ed.), 1968: *Lloyd George*. Englewood Cliffs, NJ: Prentice-Hall.

Gollin, A., 1960: The Observer *and J. L. Garvin, 1908–14*. London: Oxford University Press.

——, 1964: *Pronconsul in Politics*. London: Anthony Blond.

——, 1988: Assessing Lloyd George. *Journal of British Studies*, 27, 321–5.

Grieves, K., 1988: *The Politics of Manpower, 1914–18*. Manchester: Manchester University Press.

——, 1989: *Sir Eric Geddes*. Manchester: Manchester University Press.

——, 1991: Businessmen in wartime government. In Loades, 1991.

159

Grigg, J., 1973: *The Young Lloyd George*. London: Eyre Methuen.
——, 1974: Lloyd George and the Boer War. In Morris, 1974.
——, 1976: Liberals on trial. In Sked and Cook, 1976.
——, 1978: *Lloyd George: the people's champion, 1902–1911*. London: Methuen.
——, 1985: *Lloyd George: from peace to war, 1912–1916*. London: Methuen.
Guinn, P., 1965: *British Strategy and Politics, 1914–1918*. Oxford: Clarendon Press.
Hamer, D. A., 1972: *Liberal Politics in the Age of Gladstone and Rosebery*. Oxford: Clarendon Press.
——, 1977: *The Politics of Electoral Pressure*. Hassocks: Harvester Press.
Hankey, Lord, 1945: *Government Control in War*. Cambridge: Cambridge University Press.
——, 1961: *The Supreme Command*, 2 vols. London: Allen & Unwin.
Hay, J. R., 1975: *The Origins of the Liberal Welfare Reforms, 1906–14*. London: Macmillan.
Hazlehurst, C., 1968: The conspiracy myth. In Gilbert, 1968.
——, 1970: Asquith as Prime Minister, 1908–1916. *English Historical Review*, 85, 502–31.
——, 1971: *Politicians at War, July 1914 to May 1915*. London: Cape.
——, 1976: The part a Cabinet wife played in the bewildering fall of Asquith. *The Times*, 4 December, *p. 12*.
*Hennock, E. P., 1987: British Social Reform and German Precedents*. Oxford: Clarendon Press.
Hill, P. and Keynes, R. (eds), 1990: *Lydia and Maynard: letters between Lydia Lopokova and John Maynard Keynes*. London: Deutsch.
Hodgson, S. (ed.), 1943: *Ramsay Muir: an autobiography and some essays*. London: Lund Humphries.
Jalland, P., 1980: *The Liberals and Ireland*. Brighton: Harvester.
James, R. Rhodes (ed.), 1974: *Winston S. Churchill: his complete speeches, 1897–1963*. New York: Chelsea House.
Jeffrey, K., 1984: *The British Army and the Crisis of Empire, 1918–22*. Manchester: Manchester University Press.
Johnson, P. B., 1968: *Land Fit for Heroes*. Chicago: University of Chicago Press.
Jones, M., 1991: *A Radical Life: the biography of Megan Lloyd George, 1902–66*. London: Hutchinson.
Jones, T., 1951: *Lloyd George*. Cambridge, Mass.: Harvard University Press.
Kennedy, P. M., 1980: *The Rise of the Anglo-German Antagonism*. London, Allen & Unwin.
Kent, B., 1989: *The Spoils of War*. Oxford: Clarendon Press.
Keynes, J. M., 1919: *The Economic Consequences of the Peace*. London: Macmillan.
——, 1933: *Essays in Biography*. London: Macmillan.
Kinnear, M., 1973: *The Fall of Lloyd George*. London: Macmillan.
Koss, S., 1968: The destruction of Britain's last Liberal government. *Journal*

*of Modern History*, 40, 257–77.

Koss, S. (ed.), 1973: *The Pro-Boers*. Chicago: Chicago University Press.

——, 1975: *Nonconformity in Modern British Politics*. London: Batsford.

——, 1984: *The Rise and Fall of the Political Press in Britain*, vol. 2. London: Hamish Hamilton.

Lawlor, S., 1983: *Britain and Ireland, 1914–1923*. Dublin: Gill and Macmillan.

Lentin, A., 1984: *Lloyd George, Woodrow Wilson and the Guilt of Germany*. Leicester: Leicester University Press.

——, 1991: The treaty that never was: Lloyd George and the abortive Anglo-French Alliance of 1919. In Loades, 1991.

Lloyd George, D., 1910: *Better Times*. London: Hodder & Stoughton.

——, 1912: *The People's Insurance*, 2nd edn. London: Hodder & Stoughton.

——, 1915: *Through Terror to Triumph*. London: Hodder & Stoughton.

——, 1918: *The Great Crusade*. London: Hodder & Stoughton.

——, 1933, 1934, 1936: *War Memoirs*, 6 vols. London: Nicolson & Watson.

——, 1938: *The Truth about the Peace Treaties*. 2 vols. London: Victor Gollancz.

Lloyd George, F., 1967: *The Years that are Past*. London: Hutchinson.

Lloyd George, R., 1947: *Dame Margaret: the life story of his mother*. London: Allen & Unwin.

——, 1960: *Lloyd George*. London: Frederick Muller.

Loades, J. (ed.), 1991: *The Life and Times of David Lloyd George*. Bangor: Headstart Publications.

Lowe, P., 1971: The rise to the Premiership, 1914–16. In Taylor, 1971.

Lucy, H.W., 1905: *Later Peeps at Parliament*. London: Newnes.

McCormick, D., 1963: *The Mask of Merlin*. London: Macdonald.

McEwen, J. M., 1978: The Press and the fall of Asquith. *Historical Journal*, 21, 863–83.

——, 1981: Northcliffe and Lloyd George at war, 1914–1918. *Historical Journal*, 24, 651–72.

Machin, G. I. T., 1987: *Politics and the Churches in Great Britain: 1869–1921*. Oxford: Clarendon Press.

——, 1991: Lloyd George and nonconformity. In Loades, 1991.

Macmillan, H., 1975: *The Past Masters*. London: Macmillan.

Mallet, Sir C., 1930: *Mr Lloyd George: a study*. London: Ernest Benn.

Marder, A. J., 1961: *From Dreadnought to Scapa Flow*, vol. 1. London: Oxford University Press.

Margach, J., 1978: *The Abuse of Power*. London: W. H. Allen.

Masterman, L., 1939: *C. F. G. Masterman*. London: Ivor Nicolson & Watson.

——, 1959: Recollections of David Lloyd George. *History Today*, 9, 160–9, 274–81.

——, 1960: Reminiscences of Lib-Lab days. *New Outlook*.

Mayer, A.J., 1968: *Politics and Diplomacy of Peacemaking*. London: Weidenfeld & Nicolson.

Mills, J. Saxon, 1924: *David Lloyd George: War Minister*. London: Cassell.

Morgan, K. O., 1963(a): *David Lloyd George: Welsh Radical as world statesman*.

Cardiff: University of Wales Press.

——, 1963(b): *Wales in British Politics, 1868–1922*. Cardiff: University of Wales Press.

——, 1970: Lloyd George's premiership. *Historical Journal*, 13, 130–57.

——, 1974: *Lloyd George*. London: Weidenfeld & Nicolson.

——, 1978: 1902–1924. In *Coalitions in British Politics*, ed. D. Butler. London: Macmillan.

——, 1979: *Consensus and Disunity: the Lloyd George coalition government, 1918–1922*. Oxford: Clarendon Press.

——, 1981: *Rebirth of a Nation: Wales, 1880–1980*. Oxford Clarendon Press, and Cardiff: University of Wales Press.

——, 1988: Tom Ellis versus Lloyd George. In *Politics and Society in Wales, 1840–1922*, ed. G. H. Jenkins and J. B. Smith. Cardiff: University of Wales Press.

——, 1989: Lloyd George and the Irish. In *Ireland after the Union*, introd. R. Blake. Oxford: Clarendon Press.

——, 1991: Lloyd George and Welsh Liberalism. In Loades, 1991.

Morgan, K. O. (ed.), 1973: *Lloyd George Family Letters, 1885–1936*. Oxford: Clarendon Press, and Cardiff: University of Wales Press.

Morris, A. J., 1972: *Radicalism against War, 1906–1914*. London: Longman.

Morris, A. J. (ed.), 1974: *Edwardian Radicalism, 1900–1914*. London: Routledge & Kegan Paul.

Mowat, C. L., 1964: *Lloyd George*. London: Oxford University Press.

Murray, A. C., 1945: *Master and Brother*. London: John Murray.

Murray, B., n.d. [1932]: *L.G.* London: Sampson Low, Marston.

Murray, B. K., 1980: *The People's Budget, 1909–10*. Oxford: Clarendon Press.

——, 1990: 'Lloyd George, the Navy estimates, and the inclusion of rating relief in the 1914 Budget'. *Welsh History Review*, 15, 58–78.

Offer, A., 1981: *Property and Politics, 1870–1914*. Cambridge: Cambridge University Press.

Orde, A., 1990: *British Policy and European Reconstruction after the First World War*. Cambridge: Cambridge University Press.

Owen, F., 1954: *Tempestuous Journal: Lloyd George, his life and times*. London: Hutchinson.

Packer, I., 1991: Lloyd George and the Liberal land campaign, 1912–14. In Loades, 1991.

Peele, G. and Cook, C. (eds), (1975): *The Politics of Reappraisal, 1918–1939*. London: Macmillan.

Powell, D., 1991: Lloyd George's legacy to Liberalism. In Loades, 1991.

Price, R. E., 1975(a): Lloyd George and Merioneth politics, 1885–86. *Journal of Merioneth History and Record Society*, 7, 292–307.

——, 1975(b): Lloyd George and the election in the Caernarfon Boroughs, 1890. *Caernarvonshire Historical Society Transactions*, 36, 136–72.

——, 1983: *Megan Lloyd George*. Carnarvon: Gwynedd County Council.

Pugh, M., 1974: Asquith, Bonar Law and the first coalition. *Historical Journal*, 17, 813–36.

——, 1978: *Electoral Reform in War and Peace*. London: Routledge & Kegan Paul.

——, 1988: *Lloyd George*. London: Longman.

——, 1991: Left in the centre? Lloyd George and the centrist tradition in British politics. In Loades, 1991.

Purvey-Tyrer, N., 1991: Lloyd George, the Bishop of St Asaph and the disestablishment controversy. In Loades, 1991.

Raine, G. E., 1913: *The Real Lloyd George*. London: Allen.

——, 1914: *Lloyd George and the Land*. London: Allen.

Ramsden, J., 1978: *The Age of Balfour and Baldwin, 1902–1940*. London, Longman.

Raymond, E. T. (E. R. Thompson), 1922: *Mr Lloyd George*. London: Collins.

Rendel, Lord, 1931: *The Personal Papers of Lord Rendel*, ed. F. E. Hamer. London: Ernest Benn.

Riddell, Lord, 1933(a): *Lord Riddell's War Diary, 1914–1918*. London: Ivor Nicholson & Watson.

——, 1933(b): *Lord Riddell's Intimate Diary of the Peace Conference and After, 1918–1923*. London: Gollancz.

——, 1934: *More Pages from my Diary, 1908–1914*. London: Country Life.

——, 1986: *The Riddell Diaries, 1908–1923*, ed. J. M. McEwen. London: Athlone Press.

Robertson, J. M., 1923: *Mr Lloyd George and Liberalism*. London: Chapman & Dodd.

Roch, W., 1920: *Mr Lloyd George and the War*. London: Chatto & Windus.

Roskill, S., 1970–4: *Hankey: man of secrets*, vols 1–3. London: Collins.

Rowland, P., 1968, 1971: *The Last Liberal Governments*, 2 vols. London: Barrie & Rockliff.

——, 1975: *Lloyd George*. London: Barrie & Jenkins.

Russell, A. K., 1973: *Liberal Landslide: the General Election of 1906*. Newton Abbot: David & Charles.

Scally, R. J., 1975: *The Origins of the Lloyd George Coalition*, Princeton, NJ: Princeton University Press.

Searle, G. R., 1971: *The Quest for National Efficiency, 1899–1914*. Oxford: Basil Blackwell.

——, 1983: The Edwardian Liberal Party and business, *English Historical Review*, 98, 28–60.

——, 1987: *Corruption in British Politics, 1895–1930*. Oxford: Clarendon Press.

Shakespeare, Sir G., 1949: *Let Candles be Brought In*. London: Macdonald.

Shannon, C. B., 1988: *Arthur J. Balfour and Ireland, 1874–1922*. Washington, DC: Catholic University of America Press.

Sharp, A., 1991: Lloyd George and foreign policy, 1918–1922: the 'and yet' factor. In Loades, 1991.

Sked, A. and Cook, C. (eds), 1976: *Crisis and Controversy*. London: Macmillan.

Skidelsky, R., 1967: *Politics and the Slump*. London: Macmillan.

Spender, H., 1920: *The Prime Minister*. London: Hodder & Stoughton.

Spender, J. A. and Asquith, C., 1932: *Life of Herbert Henry Asquith, Lord Oxford and Asquith*. London: Hutchinson.

Sylvester, A. J., 1947: *The Real Lloyd George*. London: Cassell.

——, 1975: *Life with Lloyd George*. London: Macmillan.

Tanner, D., 1990: *Political Change and the Labour Party, 1900–1918*. Cambridge: Cambridge University Press.

Taylor, A. J. P., 1959: Politics in the First World War. *Proceedings of the British Academy*, 45, 67–95. (Reprinted several times, including in his *Essays in English History*. Harmondsworth: Penguin, 1976.)

——, 1961: *Lloyd George: rise and fall* (pamphlet). Cambridge: Cambridge University Press. (Reprinted several times, including in his *Essays in English History*.) Harmondsworth: Penguin, 1976.

——, 1965: *English History, 1914–1945*. Oxford: Clarendon Press.

Taylor, A. J. P. (ed.), 1971(a): *Lloyd George: twelve essays*. London: Hamish Hamilton.

——, A. J. P. (ed.), 1971(b): *Lloyd George: a diary by Frances Stevenson*. London: Hutchinson.

——, 1975: *My Darling Pussy: the letters of Lloyd George and Frances Stevenson, 1913–1941*. London: Weidenfeld & Nicolson.

Thompson, J. A., 1990: 'The historians and the decline of the Liberal Party', *Albion*, 22, 65–83.

Thomson, D., 1965: *England in the Twentieth Century*. Harmondsworth: Penguin.

Thomson, M., 1948: *David Lloyd George*. London: Hutchinson.

Townshend, C., 1975: *The British Campaign in Ireland, 1919–1921*. London: Oxford University Press.

Turner, J., 1980: *Lloyd George's Secretariat*. Cambridge: Cambridge University Press.

——, 1982: Cabinets, committees and secretariats: the higher direction of the war. In Burk, 1982.

Turner, J. (ed.), 1988: *Britain and the First World War*. London: Unwin, Hyman.

Ward, A. J., 1974: Lloyd George and the 1918 Irish conscription crisis. *Historical Journal*, 17, 107–29.

Weinroth, H. S., 1970: British Radicals and the balance of power, 1902–1914. *Historical Journal*, 13, 653–82.

——, 1971: Left-wing opposition to naval armaments in Britain before 1914. *Journal of Contemporary History*, 6, 93–120.

West, G., 1930: *Lloyd George's Last Fight*. London: Alston Rivers.

Wiemann, F. W., 1971: Lloyd George and the struggle for the navy estimates of 1914. In Taylor, 1971(a).

Wilson, T., 1966: *The Downfall of the Liberal Party, 1914—35.* London: Collins.

——, 1986: *The Myriad Faces of War.* Cambridge: Polity Press, and Oxford: Basil Blackwell.

Wilson, T. (ed.), 1970: *The Political Diaries of C. P. Scott, 1911—1928.* London: Collins.

Woodward, D. R., 1983: *Lloyd George and the Generals.* Newark: University of Delaware Press.

Wrigley, C. J., 1976: *David Lloyd George and the British Labour Movement.* Hassocks: Harvester.

——, 1982: The Ministry of Munitions: an innovatory department. In Burk, 1982.

——, 1985: Labour and the trade unions. In Brown, 1985.

——, 1990: *Lloyd George and the Challenge of Labour.* Hemel Hempstead: Harvester Wheatsheaf.

——, 1991: Lloyd George and the Labour Party after 1922. In Loades, 1991.

# Index

Cecil, Lord H., 36
Chamberlain, A., 61, 102−3, 108, 113−14
Chamberlain, J., 2, 3, 11, 12−14, 18, 36, 39, 49, 51, 59−62, 118, 129, 146, 147
Chamberlain, N., 61, 139−41, 143
Chanak crisis (1922), 115
Chaplin, H., 26
Chelmsford, Lord, 110
Churchill, Lord R., 27, 61
Churchill, W. S., 2, 8, 9, 36, 44, 47, 48, 51−2, 65, 67−8, 73, 75, 94, 109, 111−12, 114, 138, 141−5, 149, 152
Clapham, Sir J., 41
Clemenceau, G., 94, 98, 143
Cobden, R., 1, 36, 37, 57, 58, 61, 146
conscription, 73−6, 82, 105, 121
Constitutional Conference (1910), 47−8
Cowdray, Lord, 84
Craig, Sir J., 108
Cripps, Sir S., 140, 145
Cromwell, O., 29, 30, 32, 61
Crozier, W. P., 136
Cudlipp, H., 141
Cunliffe, Lord, 97, 103
Curzon, Lord, 1, 86, 115
*Cymru Fydd*, 20−2

Daniel, D. R., 43, 48
Davies, W. Watkin, 3, 12, 36−7
Davitt, M., 11, 27
Dawson of Penn, Lord, 144
Derby, Lord, 87, 108
De Valera, E., 108, 109
Devonport, Lord, 84
Dilke, Sir C., 25
Dillon, J., 27
Disciples of Christ, 7
Disraeli, B., 1, 6, 61
Dixon, E. H., 151
Dogger Bank Incident (1904), 59
Du Parcq, H., 3, 12, 62
Dyer, R. E., 110

education, 28, 30−4, 36, 39, 40, 68, 101, 102
Edward VII, King, 41, 46−7
Edwards, F., 20

Elibank, Master of, 48, 148
Ellis, T., 13, 14, 15, 16, 19
Esher, Lord, 86
Evans, S. T., 18, 21, 25

Fashoda Incident (1898), 59
First World War, 2, 23, 68−93, 105, 121, 136, 143, 149, 154
Fisher, H. A. L., 84, 101
Fisher, Sir J., 65, 72
Foch, F., 90
Fox, C. J., 64
free trade, 35−6, 40, 42−3, 119, 133−4, 148
Freeden, M., 120
French, D., 75
French, Sir J., 65
Fry, M., 64, 68
Furness, Sir C., 47

Garvin, J. L., 46, 50
Geddes, Sir E., 72, 79, 91, 102, 113
Gee, T., 9, 13
general elections
  **1880**, 9
  **1885**, 13
  **1886**, 14−15
  **1892**, 19
  **1895**, 21, 25
  **1900**, 17
  **1906**, 40
  **1910** (Jan), 46
  **1910** (Dec), 49
  **1918**, 2, 92, 96−7, 104, 105
  **1922**, 122−3
  **1923**, 123, 126, 127, 133
  **1924**, 127
  **1929**, 130, 154
  **1931**, 133
  **1935**, 134, 137−8
General Strike (1926), 104, 126−8
Genoa Conference (1922), 115, 147
George V, King, 48, 87, 89, 108
George, M. E. (sister), 7
George, W. (father), 6−7
George W. (brother), 7−8, 10, 12
George, W. (nephew), 17
Gilbert, B. B., 5, 11, 33, 36, 66, 148
Gladstone, H. (Lord), 128

167

169